Frequencies of God

Frequencies of God

*Walking Through Advent
with R. S. Thomas*

Carys Walsh

CANTERBURY
PRESS
Norwich

© Carys Walsh 2020

Published in 2020 by Canterbury Press
Editorial office
3rd Floor, Invicta House
108–114 Golden Lane
London EC1Y 0TG, UK
www.canterburypress.co.uk

Canterbury Press is an imprint of Hymns Ancient & Modern Ltd
(a registered charity)

Hymns Ancient & Modern® is a registered trademark of
Hymns Ancient & Modern Ltd
13A Hellesdon Park Road, Norwich
Norfolk NR6 5DR, UK

British Library Cataloguing in Publication data

A catalogue record for this book is available
from the British Library

978 1-78622-088-2

Typeset by Regent Typesetting

Contents

Week 3 – Journeying

Week 4 – Birthing

Week 5 – Seeing

To David

Acknowledgements

Thanks go to all those who have shared reflections and conversations about R. S. Thomas, and who have offered encouragement in the writing of this book. Particular thanks go to David Lonsdale, for his wise counsel over years of guiding me through Thomas research; Tony Brown, Emeritus Professor of the School of English, Bangor University; Mark Oakley, author and Dean of St John's College, Cambridge, for his kind support, and John Holbrook, the Bishop of Brixworth, for his generosity. Most of all, thanks to my husband David for his constant encouragement.

Introduction

R. S. Thomas

With the season of Advent, the coming of Christ is imminent, and following the contours of the season leads us through a rich time of preparation for God-with-us in the incarnation. R. S. Thomas, the Welsh priest and poet (1913–2000), is a profound and compelling guide for this season. A parish priest in Wales for all of his working life, serving in parishes on the border with England and deep in the countryside of mid-Wales, he was a prolific writer of poetry that explored his beloved homeland, the people among whom he ministered, and the beauty of the natural world. But it is for his startlingly original, prophetic and devotional religious poetry that many know him and love him. This was a long-standing strand to his work and it emerged with particular intensity when he moved to his final parish – Aberdaron – on the western-most fingertip of the Lleyn Peninsula as it reaches into the Atlantic. Thomas spoke of this as a place of arrival and belonging, where he could claim and fully inhabit his Welsh identity, and feel free to turn with a fresh intensity and focus to 'the question of the soul, the nature and existence of God'.[1]

Thomas was a writer who could draw us into the mystery of God, explore the subtleties of God's revelation, and plumb the depths of religious experience, with its struggles and joys. As a poet, he felt that he had a responsibility to 'try to experience life in all its richness, wonder and strangeness', and with his poet's craft 'to use the best language which I possess to describe that experience'.[2] And yet Thomas was always mindful that even the most deft, diverse and evocative language can never do justice to the God whom we follow. It could, however, weave and create an imaginative vision of God's kingdom, lead us into God's heartbeat, and open out the horizons of God's presence, drawing us on with a quality of breathless yearning.

This was my experience of Thomas when I first encountered his poetry many years ago. His capacity to say the unsayable and ask the unaskable, to offer silence when words do not suffice and to allow the depths of doubt to resonate with the immediacy of faith, paradoxically seemed to create so firm a foundation that I felt it could also bear the weight of my and others' questions and longings. And many years of wondering around his poetry have only deepened this conviction. His poetry has accompanied and enriched me, as I hope it will for all who hear his unique voice.

Advent Reflections

This collection of reflections on Thomas's poetry travels through the whole Advent season, and reaches into Christmas. It follows one of the many patterns of themes explored during each week of Advent: a Carmelite pattern of waiting, accepting, journeying and birthing; and to this sequence is added 'seeing', to provide focus for the final week of reflections beyond Advent. Thomas's poetry has resonances with all of these weekly themes; and the first week of our reflections, with its focus on *waiting*, follows the shifting quality of waiting to be found in Thomas's work over many years towards a depth of experience and encounter with God, which moves away from waiting 'for' and towards waiting 'upon'.

During the second week of Advent, the focus moves towards *accepting* as we reflect on acceptance of and surrender to God's presence in the world and in our lives in the midst of the ordinary, the glorious and the painful. The third week explores *journeying*, both human and divine. For Thomas, journeying included moments of stepping aside from the main path to a small side road; it included detours and moments of epiphany and surprise. And it included God's journeying in the Word made flesh, and as the 'fast God' forever before us, drawing us on.

With the fourth week, we move towards *birthing*. Thomas's meditations on the coming of Christ are shot through with the depth of love expressed through the incarnation, but also carry a poignant shadow of what was to come. Thomas's poems for the final week of *seeing* take us into the Christmas season and towards Epiphany, and offer a new, fresh glimpse of our world as a place of God's presence, even in apparent absence; even in desolation.

Reading Thomas

Thomas's poetry can lead us into a rich Advent landscape, filled with a vision of God's kingdom, both already here with us and to come. It is poetry of imminence and foretaste, presence, absence and vivid anticipation. The poetic reflections of these weeks explore these themes, and also look at how some of the poetry 'works'. It is my hope that this combination will open out his imaginative vision, enrich our reading of the poems and invite devotion as we travel through Advent.

But this also requires a kind of surrender to the poetry. The invitation, then, when reading Thomas is to linger over his language and allow its richness to do its work. And as we bring our own associations to the themes and language, there is a further invitation to let this happen, to have a conversation with the poems and allow them to speak further to us. Most of all, the invitation is to slow down, to savour the poems, hear the voice of a poet who enabled so many readers to bring their own 'Amen', and to allow the heart work of Advent to begin.

Amen. Come, Lord Jesus.

Carys Walsh
Advent 2019

WEEK I

Waiting

A voice cries out: 'In the wilderness, prepare the way of the LORD ...' (Isaiah 40.3)

Week 1 – Waiting

Day 1

The Coming

And God held in his hand
A small globe. Look, he said.
The son looked. Far off,
As through water, he saw
A scorched land of fierce
Colour. The light burned
There; crusted buildings
Cast their shadows; a bright
Serpent, a river
Uncoiled itself, radiant
With slime.
   On a bare
Hill a bare tree saddened
The sky. Many people
Held out their thin arms
To it, as though waiting
For a vanished April
To return to its crossed
Boughs. The son watched
Them. Let me go there, he said.

The Coming: The journey begins

The journey has begun. The journey in time and out of time, which will lead us through the expectation, the anticipation, the now-and-not-yet-ness of Advent, towards God-with-us at the incarnation. A one-time only journey, yet lived each year, drawing us towards the beginning of the temporal life of the eternal God, and a journey that invites us into reflection as we wait for the apocalypse – the *ap-ok-alup-tein*, the revelation, the uncovering – of God come among us.

Thomas's poem 'The Coming' marks both the ending and the beginning of the journey before us. It leads us towards the scandal of the crucifixion, but also heralds the coming of Christ into our troubled world, drawn into the heart of humanity. And it is a poem that turns our world – and our vision of it – on its axis. Rather than contemplating Christ's coming from our own perspective, we are given the vantage point of the God who gazes lovingly on us from out of time:

> And God held in his hand
> A small globe. Look, he said.

Almost as if we are watching a film, 'The Coming' seems to pan through time and eternity, inviting us into a God's-eye view of our world, and towards a particular place and time, as the Father and the Son look together 'far off, / As through water' at a broken earthly landscape. And together they see where the Son's coming is to take place; where His ending, which is not an ending, will interrupt and agitate the story of God's people. And the call is not to a glorious place, not a rich or fertile or prosperous terrain. Instead, the Father invites the Son to look at a desperate 'scorched land', with its 'crusted buildings' made bright not through benign warmth, but through fire; and it is 'slime' rather than the sun which is radiant, from the 'bright / Serpent' of a river.

This landscape, shimmering with heat and light, suggests the landscape of the Holy Land, magnetically drawing the Son to its contours. But is it *only* the Holy Land? Might this place, where the 'bright / Serpent' of a river 'radiant / With slime' seems to have lost its power to bring life, be *any* land ravaged by loss, pain or aridity – anywhere where we have confused that which is life-giving with that which may destroy? The 'bright / Serpent ... radiant / With slime' may be a clue here. And the meanings coalescing around this image reach beyond the particularity of place, and seem to draw in all of humanity – all of us. These words, which carry the echo of a snake-ruined Eden, glancing at our mixed and motley human nature, also recall impressionistically that 'as all die in Adam, so all will be made alive in Christ' (1 Corinthians 15.22).

Linger a little longer over these words and, as so often with Thomas's poetry, more emerges out of the depths. Paired with 'slime', the word 'radiant' expands to evoke more than divine or sunlit brilliance, to hint at another meaning: a place from which radiation is emitted, with all the ambivalence this suggests of the potential for both healing and destruction. So this 'Serpent, a river ... radiant / With slime' deepens the overtones of Eden, and reaches further into our human capacity for both sustaining and harming the great gift of God's creation. We are reminded that our human creativity and endeavour can not only give us wings, but also cause us to teeter on the edge of destruction, to ignore the gift of our life. For Thomas, this human potential to create and destroy, writ large in an increasingly technological age, was part of a lifetime's lament and poetic exploration. But 'The Coming' also makes clear that hope stirs and we are not alone; and that even in our tendency to embrace that which destroys, our deepest yearnings may be for life, redemption and resurrection. More than this, our deepest needs may be answered in the intense compassion of our God who draws towards us in Christ.

The yearning of Christ, echoing the human yearning for redemption, emerges as the poem pans down towards the earthly landscape. The vision changes, but again we are in a landscape that is both particular and every-place: the place of crucifixion and of an eternal human yearning for God. The Father has invited the Son to 'look' at this place, where 'On a bare / Hill a bare tree sadden[s] / The sky', but doesn't *make* Him go. Not until the Son has seen the need of the people holding out their 'thin arms' and yearning for new life and for hope in the return of 'a vanished April'; not until he has seen intimations of His own future suffering in the 'crossed / Boughs' of the tree of death which is also the tree of life does the Son of God respond. And His response is simple: 'Let me go there.' Here is the intensity of love and the unimaginable compassion of God who pours Himself out for our sakes, and inhabits the scorched land and crusted buildings; who moves among the people reaching out their thin arms to a bare hill; who responds both to our need and our rejection with equal love.

'The Coming' may be a poem of Advent, but it is more than a poem of Advent. It evokes the swooping arrival of the one who comes to be among us in this world of ordinary human pain and gorgeousness, so that our ordinary humanness is caught up in the life of God. But it also reminds us that Christ's coming to meet us in our humanity is completely wrapped up with His death in the Passion ahead, so that we might know the return of a 'vanished April'. 'The Coming' is an arc of life, death and life again, beginning with the compassionate, loving response to our need and yearning.

And if we enter into 'The Coming' at the beginning of this Advent journey, we may find the contours of our own deepest needs and cherished hopes: what are the hopes, fears, losses that would call out the love of God in our lives – in your life? What are the curious mysteries you carry, which may be laid before the coming Christ over this Advent journey, forever waiting to restore to us a vanished April, and to catch us up in His love? Asking these questions, we may begin to discern ways in which we have misunderstood that which gives life and that which distorts it. With arms held out as we await the coming of Christ and in yearning anticipation for the journey ahead, we may discover that the Christ who comes to us in the depth of compassion meets us along the way and walks with us through this time of expectant hope.

> ... The son watched
> Them. Let me go there, he said.

Week 1 – Waiting

Day 2

In a Country Church

To one kneeling down no word came,
Only the wind's song, saddening the lips
Of the grave saints, rigid in glass;
Or the dry whisper of unseen wings,
Bats not angels, in the high roof.

Was he balked by silence? He kneeled long,
And saw love in a dark crown
Of thorns blazing, and a winter tree
Golden with the fruit of a man's body.

In a Country Church

What is the quality of waiting in Advent? Unlike the more obviously penitential, and perhaps more familiar waiting of Lent, during which we recall the gone-wrongness of creation and our part in it, the waiting of Advent is a time of expectation and anticipation. Over these weeks we look forward to the presence of God with us in the incarnation; a time of hope, then, and the possibility of joy. But this does not preclude penitence and apprehension. Penitence as we again recognize those ways in which the heart's muscle closes and atrophies in the busyness of the year, or in the familiarity of faith forged in a lifetime's patterning but made almost invisible through its ubiquity. And apprehension as we wait afresh, not without trepidation for God's coming among us, with all God's uncomfortable claims upon often comfortable lives. And apprehension too as

during these weeks of waiting, we open our hearts expectantly towards a greater apprehension of the God who shares, shapes and overshadows our life.

This, then, is expectant waiting with hearts open, hopeful of a richer encounter with God, and uncertain of what this might mean for us. This is a kind of waiting that does not rush us towards an end, or offer a short cut; it is not a kind of waiting that focuses on what will come at its end. It is a crafted kind of waiting; a season of responding, attentive surrender and rootedness, as our hearts 'see their mother root', to borrow the words of another poet.[3] And this kind of waiting may take time to nurture. It may take the whole season of Advent to arrive at a kind of waiting that is more than waiting 'for', that is also a waiting 'upon', pregnant with the presence of God in the midst of anticipation.

And this kind of attentive, surrendered waiting may also be the work of a lifetime. Michael Ramsey (the Archbishop of Canterbury 1961–74) is said to have declared that he prayed for two minutes – 'but it takes me twenty-eight minutes to get there'. There are hints here of prayer's struggles, but also of an attentive waiting, which stills mind and heart so that a divine frequency breaks through, and something transformative happens. In R. S. Thomas's poetry we catch a glimpse of transformative waiting – and of transformation in waiting – which seemed to go hand in hand with his move towards interiority and silence in his middle years. While his earlier poems sometimes carry a sense of emptiness, as the years go by we find this sense of void giving way to a deepening sense of God's presence, even when God appears absent.

This is the case in his poetry of waiting, just as our own experience of waiting may change as we still ourselves to enter its currents more deeply. 'In a Country Church',[4] one of Thomas's earliest poems on this theme, has overtones of the kind of waiting that we may experience as we habituate ourselves to its moods and contours.

The opening lines of 'In a Country Church' introduce us to a solitary person waiting in the near silence of an ancient church. 'To one kneeling down', we hear, as the waiting begins, 'no

words came'. Is this because the one waiting in solitude can find no words to express their experience, or because God remains silent, apparently unresponsive? With Thomas, ambivalence leads us into a landscape of rich meaning; and so we may hover over either or both meanings, and allow ourselves to be enriched. But whatever the cause or source of verbal silence, there is still some sound to be heard, albeit the mournful, musty sound of solitude in an ancient building. There is the 'wind's song', a plaintive howl, but heard as if through the 'grave saints' depicted in stained glass around the church. And there is another distant rustling: a 'dry whisper', which is the movement of wings. But these are 'Bats not angels', another ambivalence that sometimes highlights a kind of divine absence; but also simply by referring to the angels brings the sacred before us, albeit as a distant, denied whisper.

And the waiter waits on. 'Was he balked by silence?' the poet asks, with all the rich possibilities of this word 'balk'. Perhaps the silence is a hindrance – an obstacle? Or perhaps it is God's refusal to speak. Or, with an echo of an ancient meaning of the word, this silence might be like unploughed land lying between the one waiting and God: potentially fertile and verdant, but still empty. This might cause us to ask ourselves what silent waiting is like when we put ourselves in the way of God: we might experience it as an emptiness or an obstacle, or as a place of potential or actual richness. Like the one waiting in near-silence in 'In a Country Church', we may 'kneel long', but we may or may not encounter at the end of our waiting 'love in a dark crown / Of thorns blazing'.

The nature of the vision which seems to be gifted to the one waiting in the wild emptiness of an ancient church is not clear, but the incongruous, tumbling image of the 'winter tree / Golden with the fruit of a man's body' leaves us with the paradox of divine love. The cross before the one waiting is a sign both of death and resurrection; it is a 'winter tree' that nevertheless brings forth the colours and fruit of springtime, as this death can only, *will* only, lead to life. But there is no sense that this vision – this gift – is some kind of reward; that the waiter finally does catch a glimpse of this 'winter tree / Golden with the fruit of a man's body' is a reminder that, as we wait, it is for God to offer a gift and not for us to command a reward for our waiting.

The experience of waiting in 'In a Country Church' seems to be waiting at its simplest and most difficult. There is in this brief poem a mood of worship and of solemnity; there is isolation, stillness and muffled, whispering movement, and there is the quiet yearning for God which spurs on the one waiting, who simply waits, even when the country church appears to be a place of God's absence. Here is the patience required as we embark on a time of waiting; but so too is there impatience with silence and absence, with the wind and the bats.

And so this poem – written when Thomas was yet to plunge fully into the depths of his own interior world, and before he had turned his attention 'increasingly to the question of the soul, the nature and existence of God, and the problem of time in the universe'[5] – may resonate with our own experience of patient, frustrated waiting for God. Here is waiting in a season of hard weather. Here is waiting when we are not used to its rigours. Here is waiting when we are aware of the sound of our own silence. Here is waiting 'for' rather than waiting 'upon'.

Yet our experience of waiting may be transformed by the Advent journey, as waiting itself becomes a place of God's action, and the apparent emptiness in which we sit hums with the presence of the God upon whom we wait. This may be a time of learning the contours of waiting, and recognizing that as we put ourselves in the way of God, we begin to see in the dark, and discover a presence so profound that we cannot escape it. And as we focus more and more on God's presence, we may notice the breath of God who breathes in and through us.

Week 1 – Waiting

Day 3

In Church

Often I try
To analyse the quality
Of its silences. Is this where God hides
From my searching? I have stopped to listen,
After the few people have gone,
To the air recomposing itself
For vigil. It has waited like this
Since the stones grouped themselves about it.
These are the hard ribs
Of a body that our prayers have failed
To animate. Shadows advance
From their corners to take possession
Of places the light held
For an hour. The bats resume
Their business. The uneasiness of the pews
Ceases. There is no other sound
In the darkness but the sound of a man
Breathing, testing his faith
On emptiness, nailing his questions
One by one to an untenanted cross.

In Church

Eleven years have passed since yesterday. Eleven years of reflecting on God and God's ways; of exploring the experience of God's presence and absence, and Thomas is again to be found waiting on God in 'In Church'. As the years passed, waiting began to have a different texture for Thomas. Over time, Thomas seemed to move within; he developed a kind of religious interiority which shaped and flavoured his spirituality and poetry, and shaped too how he wrote about waiting.

'In Church' shows us a glimpse of these changes. To read this poem is to discover waiting as an all-embracing experience: it is a state of being and a place of action; it is something to be engaged with, experienced and interrogated – but not alone. Thomas no longer appears as a solitary figure set against the backdrop of a church, but as one exploring a silent emptiness which occupies the building as a tangible presence. It is as if the very space in which the waiting takes place has become a fellow player in a shared experience; an almost solid object shaped by the edges and boundaries which describe its con- tours, which has its own shape and character, enveloping the kneeling figure, and reaching into nooks and crannies, prob- ing spaces, and nestling amongst stones which have 'grouped themselves about it'. This is a place of spiritual engagement, something to be explored and probed, as the questing heart reaches into the surrounding space, and the one waiting in prayer tries 'To analyse the quality / Of its silences'.

And as he waits, and lingers over this silence, Thomas's experience hovers between absence and presence. 'Is this where God hides / From my searching?' he asks, as he waits alone but not alone in the quiet of a church when the worshippers have left:

> ... I have stopped to listen.
> After the few people have gone,
> To the air recomposing itself
> For vigil. It has waited like this
> Since the stones grouped themselves about it.

Thomas is accompanied not by people, or saints long gone, but by the air itself, an ethereal but solid presence, so tangible that the 'stones grouped themselves about it'. And it waits with Thomas. In fact waiting seems to be the natural state of the air in this silent church, as it 'recompos[es] itself / For vigil'.

Vigil: a rich and multivalent word, conjuring up associations of waiting, wakefulness, watchfulness and worship. It is a word of *active* waiting before God, with overtones of engaged surrender, purposeful receptivity, and devotional presence in preparation for the holiest of times; and so it takes us into the heart of Advent waiting.

In this active waiting, Thomas and the air that he breathes, and in the presence of which he waits, appear to blur together, as if it is *he*, as well as the air, who recomposes himself for vigil 'After the few people have gone'. The stones in the church, which describe the contours of the silent air, also seem to blur together with the one who is waiting: the 'hard ribs / Of a body that our prayers have failed / To animate', may refer to the church building – but so too could it refer to Thomas and his own struggle for animation in prayer; *his* ribs, *his* body which has not been quickened by prayer as well as this place of worship. This is the struggle any one of us can have at a time of waiting, praying, reaching, demanding, and trying to surrender. But more than this, there may be echoes in Thomas's words of the very human experience that, in struggle and waiting, it is God who seems not to have been animated by the prayers of the faithful.

Thomas never sugar-coats the experience of waiting or the rigours of prayer. As he moved into waiting more deeply, more attentively and more watchfully, so too did he experience more fully the hoped-for, barely grasped state of immersive attention, and the intermittent 'signal' of God, now present in this place of prayer, now absent. Hardly surprising, then, that as time went by, the context in which waiting takes place, where God is both present in the hope of encounter, but always elusive, is no neutral backdrop, and nor does the one waiting simply wait, but responds, shifts, changes direction and allows himself to be changed and challenged. In 'In Church', the move is a marked one, from self-absorption ('Is this where God hides / From my searching?') and 'analys[is]', seemingly in an attempt to understand – to master – the silent elusiveness of God in this place of worship, towards a surrender into questioning at the end, with the waiter 'nailing his questions / One by one to an untenanted cross'. The turning-point is difficult to spot; as difficult as it is to spot when we shift from trying to master or 'domesticate' God (to use a Thomas word) to surrendering ourselves to God's mysterious encounter with us. Perhaps in this poem, the turning-point is as the air recomposes itself, and it seems that prayer has 'failed / To animate' this place, this God.

Is this a moment of realization that it is not up to *us* to animate God (the one who animates and moves us) in prayer? And as the empty space of the church shifts and retrieves the silence after the people have gone, we are perhaps left with the thought that our usual tendency, even in worship, can be to try to meet God on our terms. Now, the one waiting senses the shadows re-emerging, the 'bats resum[ing] their business', and the 'uneasiness of the pews' ceasing. The final image we are left with in 'In Church' is

> ... the sound of a man
> Breathing, testing his faith
> On emptiness, nailing his questions
> One by one to an untenanted cross.

Here, there is no resolution in a final picture of a cross 'Golden with the fruit of a man's body'. And there is no final relief from waiting and silence. Our analysis, our attempts to know and master, must cease. Meaning cannot be wrung out of the silence, nor can the God who 'hides' from the one searching be made present by demand. Now, the way is to wait, and to live with questions; and this may be uncomfortable. But, just as the naming of that which is absent immediately makes it present (a constant theme for Thomas, which deepened over time), so the untenanted cross resonates with the absent Christ. And it is not a sense of resolution that is significant, nor any answering of the questions asked by the one waiting, but the process of sitting with the unanswered questions, drawn close to the untenanted cross, the place of endless mystery, endless questions and fathomless answers. Simply putting oneself in the way of God ushers in a new texture of experience.

There is, in this poem, a deepening sense of silence and of waiting, in the movement from analysis at the beginning, to questioning at the end, by way of absence, listening, waiting, encounter, acceptance, surrender, questioning. As we habituate ourselves to the practice of waiting this Advent, and allow ourselves to enter into its depths and eddies, we may discover ourselves trying to keep control of the experience, and of how we expect God to meet us. But we may find that waiting takes on a life of its own, and experience our surroundings not as neutral places, but externalizations of our inner experience. Or we may catch glimpses of the God upon whom we wait, who, if 'hid[ing] from [our] searching', *must* be present.

And we may find that as we allow the waiting to break over us, discover its riches, and experience the texture of the space around us, its movements, its contours and its sounds, we understand our world more fully as a place of God's grace and gift. This is the experience of leaning into the God who surrounds us and is the air that we breathe, so that even as we hover between knowing and not knowing God's presence, so too do we hover between waiting and knowing ourselves already to have been met.

Week 1 – Waiting

Day 4

Kneeling

Moments of great calm,
Kneeling before an altar
Of wood in a stone church
In summer, waiting for the God
To speak; the air a staircase
For silence; the sun's light
Ringing me, as though I acted
A great role. And the audiences
Still; all that close throng
Of spirits waiting, as I,
For the message.
       Prompt me, God;
But not yet. When I speak,
Though it be you who speak
Through me, something is lost.
The meaning is in the waiting.

Kneeling

Reading 'Kneeling',[6] savouring its moods and cadences, is to enter deeply into the heart of Advent waiting. This brief and intensely atmospheric poem, which emerged at a time when Thomas was turning 'increasingly to the question of the soul, the nature and existence of God, and the problem of time in the universe',[7] has become one of his most celebrated poems of waiting, silence and revelation. As Thomas was drawn increasingly into the interior, and as he dropped within in prayer, so too did God become the protagonist in his poetry, an object and subject of reflection, and a constant presence even in loquacious silence.

This is a poem of both extraordinary simplicity and extraordinary depth, speaking of the God who comes among us in the physicality of our lives, who fills the spaces around us, and who quickens the silences. Walking slowly through the poem with prayerful attention and lingering over its images, paradoxes and associations, we can mine its riches and be nourished by the spirituality which emerges through it. So there is the encouragement to *wait* for the images to reach you as you read 'Kneeling': to read it in the spirit of a poem that tells us that 'The meaning is in the waiting'.

The language of the poem has an elegant clarity which immediately sets a tone of stillness, even though Thomas seems to begin as if he is already halfway through a sentence or a thought. There is calm as the protagonist kneels 'before an altar / Of wood', and waits for 'the God' to speak. This may be summertime, as we are told, but these first few lines also present us with the sense of timelessness within time, which is one of the hallmarks of this poem. 'Moments of great calm' could be moments in the immediacy of Thomas's experience, or an eternity of moments experienced in that place, and so we are in the presence of time sliding and slipping, eternally moving and undeniably 'now'. The simple physicality of the scene is underlined by Thomas drawing our attention to the 'altar / Of wood in a stone church'. This is solid and real and immediate, and speaks to us of God's presence in the ordinary physicality of life, in the ordinary interior of the tiny church of St Maelrhys, where Thomas knelt in prayer.

But then the mood shifts, just slightly, and this place of waiting becomes transfigured as Thomas kneels, waiting for 'the God' to speak. This is an often-repeated way for Thomas to name God, and it shimmers with a sense of the ancient, the solid, the eternal, with the sacred reaching deeply into the Christian past and into the primordial landscape of the stone church. But this solidity is also shot through with an ethereal, transfiguring quality of light, 'a staircase / For silence', seeming to be a transit point, a place of movement between earth and heaven, constant, shifting and shimmering. The unmistakable echoes of Jacob's ladder also bring to mind God's presence, even when we are unaware of it, and deepen the sense in 'Kneeling' of one waiting for God and yet learning that it is in the very waiting that God is discovered. 'Surely the Lord is in this place – and I did not know it!', says Jacob, waking from his reverie,[8] as Thomas too might say.

In 'Kneeling', language is carefully used and images crafted to hold together the 'ordinary' and the sacred in a single experience. Solidity and translucence, the immediate moment and eternity, presence and absence are all brought together, and by simply placing the words 'silence' and 'sound' one above the other, we are held in an experience of silent communication:

> ... waiting for the God
> To *speak*; the air a staircase
> For *silence*;

The transfigured ordinary also extends to the one waiting, who is haloed, or surrounded in the 'sun's light', 'as though' he acts a great role. This 'as though' is tantalizing in its meaning. In this context, Thomas does indeed have a role as priest,[9] a pray-er, and as someone waiting upon God. But it is a semi-playful comment, with Thomas seeming to say: 'it's as if I'm in the spotlight!'– and so the 'great role' is deliberately undermined, and we are witnessing the transfiguration of the ordinary, and the everyday-ness of the sacred. But the image of Thomas acting a 'great role' carries on as he waits in the presence of 'audiences'. These may be members of the congregation, for whom Thomas mediates God's word and presence, or they may be the saints; the ancient souls of this ancient outcrop of land, on the westernmost tip of the Lleyn Peninsula, reaching out into the Atlantic with the delicacy of a spring branch and the solidity of iron. All are waiting for 'the message'.

And then the line breaks.

Prompt me, God;
But not yet. When I speak,
Though it be you who speak
Through me, something is lost.
The meaning is in the waiting.

Though two-thirds of the way through the poem, this is per-
haps the pivotal moment, signalling another shift in mood, and
taking us into the heart of waiting as a place of God's action.
The mood and atmosphere of silent waiting have been care-
fully set, and the church has shimmered into life, as home to
the 'close throng / of spirits', in the presence of God and the
congregation. And now, with an echo of Augustine, Thomas
prays: 'Prompt me, God; / But not yet'. The request, familiar to
so many who pray, is for God to bring an end to the waiting
by providing the words to speak; and Thomas is all too aware
that, though it might be *through* him that God speaks, when
the communication comes, he will not be able to do justice to
the source of speech. Here we see the sweet tension to be found
in waiting for something that is only received *in* and *through*
the waiting.

The experience of waiting that emerges from 'Kneeling' is
different again from that of either 'In Church' or 'In a Country
Church'. In these early days of Advent, to read all three poems
can lead us through a pattern of ever-deepening waiting, as we
settle into the moods of waiting, through solitude, interrogating
our surroundings, questioning, and towards the surrendered
waiting of 'Kneeling'. There is no anxiety in this waiting; nor
is it something to be endured or suffered. There is simply the
understanding that waiting upon God is fundamental to know-
ing God, and so Thomas opens up the paradoxical possibility
that God might be revealed while we are waiting for God to
be revealed.

None of this is to turn waiting – or the waiting of 'Kneeling'
– into an overly benign and safe experience. As we read the
poem, allow it to speak to us and allow ourselves to wait upon
God, we may find ourselves discovering that there is a tightrope
of desire and longing to be walked, which calls out from us a

depth of yearning for God, and demands focus and surrender as we teeter between longing for God to speak and knowing that as we wait, we know God more.

In 'Kneeling', the 'meaning' really is 'in the waiting'.

Week 1 – Waiting

Day 5

Suddenly

As I had always known
he would come, unannounced,
remarkable merely for the absence
of clamour. So truth must appear
to the thinker: so, at a stage
of the experiment, the answer
must quietly emerge. I looked
at him, not with the eye
only, but with the whole
of my being, overflowing with
him as a chalice would
with the sea. Yet was he
no more here than before,
his area occupied
by the unhaloed presences.
You could put your hand
in him without consciousness
of his wounds. The gamblers
at the foot of the unnoticed
cross went on with
their dicing; yet the invisible
garment for which they played
was no longer at stake, but worn
by him in this risen existence.

Suddenly[10]

After the 'moments of great calm, waiting for the God to speak' in 'Kneeling', today's poem 'Suddenly' describes the experience of God becoming surprisingly, expectedly and quietly present. And although several years divide the two different poems, 'Suddenly' could almost be read as a companion to 'Kneeling', the one describing waiting upon God in stillness and patient acknowledgement that God meets us in silent waiting, and the other a poem of being greeted in the middle of a reverie of waiting, by the sudden, natural experience of God emerging. Or, perhaps, in 'Suddenly', we are able to catch a glimpse of the 'meaning' which emerges 'in the waiting'.

If this is the poem's gift to us, it is in part given through the layered language, with its myriad associations, which leave us with a sense of God's presence suffusing our every experience. But the reality of God's presence may only be apparent to us when, through the ripeness of waiting, we discover the world in a fresh, new way; when our vision gradually shifts focus, just for a moment, and when, instead of dominating the act of seeing into the world, we can allow ourselves to be seen *through*. But this shift in focus can take time as we habituate ourselves to a new, surrendered way of seeing: the meaning is in the waiting.

In its rich evocation of such an experience, 'Suddenly' is a striking example of how a new vision of our world might sometimes open up to us as our focus shifts and when the waited for, waited upon God emerges, even if only briefly, and when we discover that the God for whom we are waiting is forever present, yet so ubiquitous that we do not notice. This is a moment of epiphany which is both surprising and obvious; that moment when the air, humming with God's presence, resolves into a new experience. But as usual, this moment of epiphany, for all that it seems to hover in the air, emerges in and through the physical world, and also in and through the careful craft of the poet. As we linger over the language of 'Suddenly' and allow it to 'overflow' us, we may not only find Thomas's words resonating with some of our own experiences, but we may also discover something of the craft of this poet, who was a seer-into-things, and used language to refract shards of light, or to communicate a sense of 'heaven in ordinarie', as George Herbert might have it.[11]

One of Thomas's greatest poetic gifts was that he could evoke so subtle and so powerful a sense of God's presence without ever naming God, as in 'Suddenly'. The luminous language, the richness of metaphor and the range of associations combine to bring God before us as if we had been waiting upon God and suddenly discovered that He is always, was always, there. As in 'Kneeling', the poem opens as if we are dropping into a flow of speech already going on. Curiously, in 'Suddenly', the opening lines of the poem have the feel of an aside, a comment added to an explanation being given of God's apparent arrival. So the meaning is not immediate or explicit, and it lacks a verb to help us decide what is going on. Instead, we are left with a beginning that seems to trail, so that its meaning tiptoes up to us as we read, echoing the unobtrusive entrance made by the divine, with its 'absence / of clamour'. There is no fanfare here, but a sense of God both profoundly present and unobtrusive, seeping into consciousness as if the one conscious has found their gaze suddenly refocused.

As the poem moves on, we are offered a picture of something real but somehow intangible, emerging into full view as the world around becomes saturated with the life at its heart, like an old-fashioned magic painting book, colouring itself in. But this drawing of something into focus takes place 'not with the eye / only', but with the 'whole ... being'. Thomas's response to that which is being revealed involves the *whole* of him, and he is engulfed by this emerging sense of God. Using imagery which reminds us of Holy Communion, Thomas talks of 'overflowing with / him as a chalice would / with the sea'. This God comes into focus and cannot be contained; God both fills Thomas who is caught up in the encounter, and spills everywhere, beyond the bounds of the poet.

And as Thomas says:

> ... Yet was he
> no more here than before,
> his area occupied
> by the unhaloed presences.

This is a curious section; it plays with ideas of how and where God is to be found in the world. God seems more present, because of the experience of 'quietly emerg[ing]', but God is not more present: 'no more here than before'. The 'unhaloed presences' suggest *us* – ordinary mortals – living in the physicality of the created world, which is also God's space. But unlike us, God cannot be 'named' as 'here' or 'not here'; God is not an additional thing in the world, but is at the heart of the world, emerging through the everyday. 'His area', which is everywhere, is 'occupied' by the ordinary people of the world, even as God is present in it. In 'Suddenly' God is not displaced by humanity or anything else in the physical world; God is the sea in which all things swim, but it takes waiting and surrender for this to become deeply known. The God who emerges is always everywhere, says Thomas; but at times we are more habituated to Him, more attuned to His frequencies, more receptive, attentive, surrendered to the divine humming in the wires. And we may be left scratching our heads as we struggle to articulate the experience of the waited-upon God breaking upon us as we find ourselves overflowing in wonder towards God.

As the images unfold towards the end of the poem, we are drawn even more deeply into Christ's presence in the world, as we are shown a glimpse of the Passion:

> You could put your hand
> in him without consciousness
> of his wounds. The gamblers
> at the foot of the unnoticed
> cross went on with
> their dicing.

As the scene of the crucifixion opens out, there is a hint that we are always living in the midst of Christ's presence, but 'without consciousness'. The story is somehow still happening and is always happening, and the reference to the soldiers gambling for Christ's clothes 'at the foot of the unnoticed / cross' hints even more that the presence of Christ in the world overshadows everything, and yet people remain unaware; the cross goes 'unnoticed'. Or perhaps the 'unhaloed presences' are aware of it in a very limited sense, as the soldiers appear to be here: playing dice for Christ's clothes, they are in touch with the presence of God in the world, but fail to notice the cross and all it means – all He means.

And as the soldiers gamble, it is as if time collapses: 'the invisible / garment for which they played', we are told, 'was no longer at stake, but worn / by him in this risen existence'. The past events become part of everyday life and in the poem's final words, 'this risen existence', the extra dimension of Christ's presence in the world quietly breaks through ordinary vision and experience, and is to be found at the heart of life. Part of the mystery of Advent is that time collapses. We are waiting again for that which has happened, which also happens continually and will happen again at some unspecified time. Christ has already come among us, His risen life 'oveflow[s] with / him as a chalice would / with the sea', and we look too for His coming again.

Week 1 – Waiting

Day 6

Suddenly

Suddenly after long silence
he has become voluble.
He addresses me from a myriad
directions with the fluency
of water, the articulateness
of green leaves; and in the genes,
too, the components
of my existence. The rock,
so long speechless, is the library
of his poetry. He sings to me
in the chain-saw, writes
with the surgeon's hand
on the skin's parchment messages
of healing. The weather
is his mind's turbine
driving the earth's bulk round
and around on its remedial
journey. I have no need
to despair; as at
some second Pentecost
of a Gentile, I listen to the things
round me: weeds, stones, instruments,
the machine itself, all
speaking to me in the vernacular
of the purposes of the One who is.

Suddenly[12]

As we weave our way through Advent, we may become
attuned to the posture of waiting and familiar with its subtle
ties and gentle light and shade. Perhaps we might experience
God drawing close, appearing over the horizon of our prayers
– and then perhaps seeming to become distant again, only to
return, quietly nudging us and appearing at the corner of our
eye. If so, we might be surprised by today's poem, the second
that Thomas called 'Suddenly'. If his first 'Suddenly' is charac-
terized by God becoming surprisingly, expectedly and quietly
present, in the second, published eight years later, God's
presence appears explosive. 'Suddenly, after long silence', we
hear – after a long time when God was not to be heard, and
perhaps a long time of waiting – God arrives with clamour, as
a turbulent, joyous and almost brazen tumbling of experiences
through the natural world. It is as if this long time of silence
has prepared the ears of the one waiting to be unstopped,
as Thomas 'hears' his silent God who has suddenly 'become
voluble'. But this is more than a heightened sense of physical
hearing; it is a complete experience of God speaking in the
texture of the natural world, in the bits and bytes of human
life, and in the humming of the air. And this is all communi-
cated in raucous speed, in fast words, dense images, and simple
sounds which enhance the sense of urgency and immediacy.
And together, in a slightly uncharacteristic mode for Thomas,
they communicate an unfathomable, breathless joy; the joy of
the one waiting being simply overwhelmed by God-with-us.

This is a poem that deserves to be read carefully, line by line,
savouring the individual images as they arise. And as in other
poems, the style in 'Suddenly' (1983) is paradoxical. Again,
God is not named, but pervades the poem, pouring out of
cross-grained images and densely knitted metaphors; this is a
divine encounter that can only be described through language
that is rooted in our world, but also leaves us scratching our
heads, and knowing that we are reaching beyond usual experi-
ence. As early as the opening lines, the poet, the one who has
been waiting, introduces us to the shock of God's presence,

moving quickly from 'silence' at the end of the first line, to 'voluble' at the end of the second. Then he explores, through a richly textured, extended series of images, the pouring out of God's language − God's word − in our midst. We catch a glimpse of Thomas's excited surprise that his experience of absence and silence, so often explored in his poetry, has been confounded by a sense of God's chattering presence, transfiguring the natural world, which remains itself (rock remains rock and grass remains grass), and yet is also transfigured through images of sound. The natural world becomes God's world: the carrier of the words of God, and the world of God.

And so the 'fluency of water' brings the sound of a tumbling stream to mind, but suggests too that God reaches into every nook and cranny, saturating our world. Green leaves are 'articulate', verdant, vivid, filling the countryside with the murmur of their creator. Rock is the 'library' of God's poetry, a bearer and teller of God's histories in the world, in the marks, in its striations, contours and layers, suggesting wisdom emanating from the depths of time in the pre-Cambrian rock of the Lleyn Peninsula. For the most part, this is not the language of feeling but, again paradoxically, we are surrounded in 'Suddenly' (1983) with intense experience, expressed through myriad 'things': the objective, the solid, the nameable (rocks, skin, weather, leaves, weeds, stones), and even through things mistrusted by the poet: machines, turbines, instruments. All suddenly spring into longed-for, long-awaited life, and the sound of God in the world is almost deafening. It is as if everything speaks of God and God speaks through everything to Thomas, from the tiniest and most particular elements of the created world (the genes) to the greatest. The weather itself, in all its noise and churn, is 'his mind's turbine', an immense force powering the earth's movement on its axis, and on its journey towards healing − its *remedial* / journey'.

And in the midst of this nestles another image of hearing and of healing which is both sharp and gentle, carrying echoes of God's word as 'living and active, sharper than any two-edged sword' (Hebrews 4.12).

> ... He sings to me
> in the chain-saw, writes
> with the surgeon's hand
> on the skin's parchment messages
> of healing.

God can be heard in the harshest of blades, and yet too God speaks through the kindest cut of the surgeon, through whom there are 'messages of healing', wrought in human flesh. Healing again. The overwhelming presence of the God who has come in this second 'Suddenly' is a healing presence.

This world made suddenly alive speaks of the God who brings life, who is always among us, and who comes again in the incarnation. And the experience of the one who has waited upon God, is of 'some second Pentecost / of a Gentile', hearing clearly the newly understandable, exuberant, profligate, self-giving God, poured out among the most unlikely of us. The image dances with the suddenness of the Day of Pentecost and also God's Spirit poured out among the unexpected and un-expecting Gentiles.[13] Here is all the astonishment at God's profligacy, and the tumbling, pouring speech of God in language suddenly so familiar that hearers can grasp it, and know it as their own. 'Weeds, stones, instruments', we hear, even

> the machine itself, all
> speaking to me in the vernacular
> of the purposes of the One who is.

It as is if the physical world in 'Suddenly' (1983) not only carries the words of God, but also translates them, so that we discover God in the 'vernacular'. This is the eternal word embedded in the everyday and speaking to us, in a way we can grasp, of 'the purposes of the One who is'. The echoes here of the creative Word of God, spoken into the world in Christ (the 'material word', to borrow a term from Rowan Williams), again lead us more deeply into Advent. In 'Suddenly' (1983) we are invited to reflect on the incarnate word, enfleshed in matter, in weather, in the skill of humanity, and in the 'remedial journey' towards healing.

Waiting can surprise us. It may be quiet, attentive, hopeful. It may also be interrupted with an intensity of experience so immense that we find ourselves spoken to all around us. This God for whom we wait reaches us, speaks to us in myriad ways, bringing our world to life, and endowing even rocks, even water, even the most unlikely of our surroundings, with a voice that tells us that the God for whom and upon whom we wait is present. 'Suddenly' (1983) invites us into the possibility that waiting shifts our perspective to hear a world made noisy by God, where senses tumble together, and the Living Word speaks. In today's waiting, then, we may find, through the stillness, that our surroundings speak to us, and that, as for Thomas, the whisper of God come among us may become a roar.

Week 1 – Waiting

Day 7

Sea-watching

Grey waters, vast
     as an area of prayer
that one enters. Daily
     over a period of years
I have let the eye rest on them.
Was I waiting for something?
     Nothing
but that continuous waving
     that is without meaning
occurred.
     Ah, but a rare bird is
rare. It is when one is not looking,
at times one is not there
     that it comes.
You must wear your eyes out,
as others their knees.
     I became the hermit
of the rocks, habited with the wind
and the mist. There were days,
so beautiful the emptiness
it might have filled,
     its absence
was as its presence; not to be told
any more, so single my mind
after its long fast,
     my watching from praying.

Sea-watching

We are reaching the end of this first week of Advent, a week in which we have explored the textures of waiting. And these have changed and shifted over the week, as we have been invited by the poetry of Thomas to enter a silent space with no expectation for our God to appear in any prescribed form or to 'reward' our waiting. The invitation has simply been to allow our experience and our expectations to be transformed: from waiting for, towards waiting upon the God who was and is and is to come; from being the lead act in our drama of waiting, towards knowing ourselves as uniquely beloved bit-players in God's eternal presence. From experiencing quiet or space as emptiness, towards knowing all our waiting to be places and spaces of God's action. And in the waiting, our perspectives may have begun to shift, and our gaze become receptive. Ears may have been unstopped, and the stillness may have been quickened. And we may be met with God's presence in simple silence, in quiet murmurings of the empty church, the clamour of nature, the turbulence of wind and weather, and in our own hearts, unclasping in recognition that our lives are held by the one we wait upon.

In the final poem of this week, the texture of waiting again changes. After the gushing, turbulent, surprisingly vocal God of 'Suddenly' (1983), we return to a more characteristic Thomas in 'Sea-watching', a poem of God's presence and absence, and of the natural world. But in its rich and evocative images, this poem also brings together the many moods of waiting over this week. 'Sea-watching' is not overtly a poem about God, or about waiting on God. It is an extended reflection on watching water and birds in the natural world, patient, immense and unfathomable; and this experience becomes indistinguishable from the experience of waiting on God in prayer. Unlike the language of 'Suddenly' (1983), the language of 'Sea-watching' has, for the most part, a kind of languor about it, which causes us to slow down, to still ourselves, as we read or speak it out loud. And as we slow down, we share the experience of patient bird-watching (a favourite pastime of Thomas) over a cold Welsh sea. 'Grey waters', Thomas begins,

> ... vast
> as an area of prayer
> that one enters. Daily
> over a period of years

Sounds lengthen and dip, words fall away (grey, area, prayer) and lines are divided to slow our reading – or later on, to emphasize ideas, images, moods, so that the poem itself shapes its own meaning, and shapes our reading and our understanding of it. The break, for instance, between 'Daily' and 'over a period of years' highlights immediacy and habit, but also reinforces that it is a lifetime's work to watch and pray. Simply looking at the shape of the poem on the page offers a focus for reflection and meditation: indented lines flex the mood, and punctuate descriptions with reminders that solitude and absence are part of the focused surrender of waiting in sea-watching and in prayer.

> Was I waiting for something?
> Nothing
> but that continuous waving
> that is without meaning
> occurred.

'Nothing' is awaited by the poet. Or rather, 'Nothing / but', and this 'but' flips the solitary word 'Nothing' into a kind of something – into the 'continuous waving / that is without meaning', which could signify or hint at many things. The waves of the sea might come to mind; or airwaves – those frequencies humming in the air which form so strong a motif in Thomas's poems. Or perhaps we are waving to attract God's attention, or this 'continuous waving', gratuitous, with no angle and no meaning, might suggest the lapping of the sea as the continuity of God, endlessly present, endlessly meeting us, but whom we can no more pin down in place than meaning, and no more pin down and control than the sea. And yet, in the midst of this waiting for 'nothing / but that continuous waving', the one waiting is met by the unbidden glimpse of God, the 'rare bird', who surprises the watcher and waiter with its unpredictable self-revelation:

Ah, but a rare bird is
rare. It is when one is not looking,
at times one is not there
that it comes.

We may be reminded again of Ramsey's two minutes in the
company of his long-awaited God; or we may be reminded
of our own experiences of waiting upon God, only for God's
presence to reach us suddenly, unbidden, when the waiting has
stopped, or when we were thinking about something else. Or
we may simply be reminded that we cannot shape or determine
how or when the 'rare bird' happens upon us; we cannot make
it arrive by looking, any more than we can make God appear to
us by waiting and praying. We are called to wait and pray and
watch, and go beyond our waiting and praying and watching,
to a place of surrender, 'wearing out' eyes and knees, clothed in
the experience of waiting like the poem's 'hermit of the rocks'
is clothed, and like the rocks are clothed, in wind and mist.

Towards the end of the poem, the waiting in 'wind and mist'
swoops and capsizes us. 'There were days,' we are told, 'so
beautiful the emptiness / it might have filled, its absence / was as
its presence'. The one waiting discovers the beauty in the sheer
act of waiting, so intensely that even when the reason for the
waiting (whether 'rare bird' or God) seems absent, the beauti-
ful emptiness tips over into presence. There is meaning in the
waiting, and ultimately, watching and praying become indis-
tinguishable: they cannot be 'told' one from another. Watching
for the 'rare bird' over the sea, for God in the torrents and
eddies of our prayer, *is* to pray.

In 'Sea-watching', watching, praying, waiting collapse to-
gether, and waiting has become a core experience of all of life.
This is waiting upon, but also an attitude of waiting which is
so fundamental that it is also *not* waiting, but simply living.
Waiting has been stretched to an acknowledgement that the
whole of life is lived in relationship with our God who has
come among us and will come among us again at Christmas.
As we wait, we live. As we live, we wait.

WEEK 2

Accepting

Mary said, 'Here am I, the servant of the Lord; let it be with me according to your word.' Then the angel departed from her. (Luke 1.38)

Week 2 – Accepting

Day 1

Amen

And God said: How do you know?
And I went out into the fields
At morning and it was true.

Nothing denied it, neither the bowed man
On his knees, nor the animals,
Nor the birds notched on the sky's

Surface. His heart was broken
Far back, and the beasts yawned
Their boredom. Under the song

Of the larks, I heard the wheels turn
Rustily. But the scene held;
The cold landscape returned my stare;

There was no answer. Accept; accept.
And under the green capitals,
The molecules and the blood's virus.

Amen

In this second week of reflections, our attention turns to 'acceptance'. But acceptance of what? In the poetry of R. S. Thomas, any acceptance is not a simple passive response to all that happens in the world. Nor is it an easy acceptance of faith, or even of self. The acceptance that Thomas offers us is born of asking difficult questions of life, of God and of himself. Ultimately (if such a word can be used of Thomas's poetry) it is a reflection of a radical surrender of any attempt to 'domesticate' God, as Thomas might have put it, and of our own carefully constructed persona. Acceptance, for Thomas, is rooted in prayer, observation, questioning, acknowledgement of our own folly and frailty, and of God's presence in all that is absurd, tragic or uncomfortable in life, as well as the beautiful, grace-filled and joyful.

This is a kind of acceptance that is suited to the Advent season. In the surrender of waiting upon God and preparing for the coming of Christ, we are called to lay down pre-conceived understandings of how we are met by God, and experience afresh the vibrancy of God's presence, the divinely haunting hum of absence, and ourselves in the waiting and being met. Acceptance at its most radically surrendered is also at the heart of Mary's story and so at the very heart of Advent and the weeks into Christmas and Epiphany. From the acceptance of the call to be God-bearer, with the words 'Here am I, the servant of the Lord; let it be with me according to your word' (Luke 1.38), to receiving, treasuring and pondering the words of the shepherds at Christ's birth (Luke 2.19), and through to the discovery of her child as the world's lightning conductor, revealing truth, shaping destinies, exposing the heart, Mary is called to accept a life utterly shaped in God's life. And this is no easy acceptance: a sword, she is told, will pierce her soul in this God-filled, surrendered life (Luke 2.34–35). To accept this is no easy passivity.

Mary's acceptance slipped the bonds of time: she is accepting what is to come, as well as her present, and at each step of acceptance, she sees a little further ahead and a little more of the picture. This unexpected child will be called Son of God, He will be the Messiah, and He will be a light for all people, not only her own. She is perplexed, she treasures, she ponders, she is amazed at God's life unfolding within her and reaching into the future with no guarantee of comfort, and a reinterpretation of God's grace in the present.

And this may be some of the quality of acceptance we are

called to foster in Advent. We are called to live in its 'now', but with the anticipation of God-with-us hovering at the corner of our eye, and with the memory of God come among us in our midst. This can also be to accept that God-with-us may not look like the picture we carry, even unbidden, in our minds. Without even realizing it, we may tend to assume that God is more with us in the sanitized moments of life; in beauty, in the richness of life, in the gifts we have been given, or in moments of blessing and good fortune. But, as Mary knew, where heaven and earth meet, God joins us in our ordinary humanity, entering into its depth rather than lifting us out of our world. And so in fostering acceptance, we may discover God in present strangeness, absurdity and downright discomfort as well as in gift; in a dimension of depth in our world which we access, acknowledge, or accept only rarely. This is the acceptance of Advent. This is the tone of acceptance that we discover in Thomas's poetry.

The first two poems in this week of acceptance come from the same collection: *Pietà*, published in 1966. This collection emerged as Thomas was exploring in his poetry a move within, towards the depth of life and faith, and it includes poetry that explores his interior landscape, reflects on his spiritual understanding and on his relationship with God. But 'Amen' was still a rare poem at this stage of Thomas's poetic life. It contains an exchange with God that seems like both inner-world reflection and a response to God's presence in the hill farms of his parishes. Up to this point in his poetry, Thomas had often questioned the life of the hill farmer through characters, like one he named Iago Prytherch,[14] but here, in 'Amen', Thomas reflects more overtly on God's presence in the demanding life of the hill farm; inner and outer come together, in a carefully shaped poem of gradual acceptance of God in this most material of worlds.

This, though, is no country idyll. The poem opens with a challenge from God to Thomas – and to us: 'How do you know?' We may each have a different idea about what it is we are being asked: how do we know that God is with us? That there is more to life than we see? How do we trust God?

How do we know that even in the most ordinary of places God is to be found? For Thomas, the answer is simply to observe the world in which he is placed; from the sweeping fields to the infinitesimally small building blocks of 'molecules' and the 'blood's virus', reaching into the deepest level of materiality, he simply finds that 'it was true'. And yet the world on which Thomas looks is bleak: the farmer is 'bowed', the 'beasts yawn', the landscape is 'cold', and 'Amen' is shot through with hints of God both absent and present. It is an ambivalent picture, in which, while the bleak landscape does not resound with God's presence, 'Nothing denie[s] it'.

Perhaps the key point of the poem is in the central verse, which begins with 'Surface' and ends with 'Under the song', as if moving to a new level. But this is not an obvious movement from surface bleakness to a sacred foundation. The immediate, the surface, is a mottled picture of bleakness and beauty in the 'bowed man' and the 'song / of the larks', and what lies beneath, it seems, is just as mottled. The 'bowed man' in no way negates the presence of God, and yet 'Under the song / of the larks' the 'wheels turn / Rustily'. Surface and depth seem interchangeable; both reveal life and both reveal bleakness, and the call is not to answer, or to prove, or to scratch our heads over a puzzle to be solved, but to accept – both the 'molecules' and the 'blood's virus'.

The acceptance reflected in 'Amen' has a depth to it which speaks of struggle rather than serenity. It a kind of acceptance through gritted teeth, as if Thomas is *willing* himself to accept this motley world and different sense of God's economy. Perhaps here he is reflecting some kind of dissonance between head and heart, as he struggles with questions about just how much to accept, just how doggedly to persist in the idea of God with us in all that is bleak, and just how much to lament. And yet, perhaps this a feature of acceptance: that it can include lament and struggle, and may be a precursor to change or challenge inside us, or in our world. Acceptance of what is, is always the necessary first step in moving towards what will be, and the call to 'accept' embraces both bleakness and lark song, down to the mixed building blocks of life, the 'molecules and the blood's virus'. And so in 'Amen', Thomas is presenting us with an acceptance of God as the heart of the world which does not deny struggle, and does not declare that a painful surface masks a divinely golden and healed interior. This is an ambivalent and complex vision which asks us not to slip into easy acceptance, or easy dismissal of where we might find God. Our saviour is in the stable, in the byre, as well as in glory; our saviour is in rust and feathers and bent bones, as much as in the flight of the skylark, bright blossom and the fresh dawn.

Week 2 – Accepting

Day 2

This to do

I have this that I must do
One day: overdraw on my balance
Of air, and breaking the surface
Of water go down into the green
Darkness to search for the door
To myself in dumbness and blindness
And uproar of scared blood
At the eardrums. There are no signposts
There but the bones of the dead
Conger, no light but the pale
Phosphorous, where the slow corpses
Swag. I must go down with the poor
Purse of my body and buy courage,
Paying for it with the coins of my breath.

This to do

My first encounter with the poem 'This to do' was a shock. It appeared, like 'Amen', in the middle of a transitional decade in Thomas's poetry, shot through with themes old and new: Welsh hill-farming life, memories of parishioners and family, tumbling alongside deepening themes of wrestling with God. So encountering a poem of transition, as this is, need not have been such a surprise – but *this* poem shone out as starkly different. What I met in 'This to do' was a bold, immediate self-examination; courageous and daring, but also with a haunting, dreamlike quality, and an ending at once open-ended, bleak and profoundly hopeful.

In 'This to do', it is as if Thomas turns to face and address the reader – you and me – directly for the first time: 'I have this that I must do / One day', he says. It is as if he must change focus, away from constructing and towards recognition and acceptance of who he is. 'I have been describing my world, my life and my God', he seemed to be saying, 'and now I have to find and face myself. And it will mean risking my life.' By the time he wrote 'This to do', Thomas had moved to his final parish, Aberdaron, after years of moving further into Wales, in search for what he paradoxically thought of as the real Wales of his imagination.[15] But he had also been searching for a place that would help to deepen and strengthen his sense of identity (which he said 'had been weak from the start')[16] and meet the yearning he had to live and integrate his Welshness.

Now in Aberdaron, he 'learned that Welsh was the language of the majority of the parishioners, the flowing and open language of the Lleyn Peninsula',[17] and so he felt that here he had 'reached the destination of his own pilgrimage'.[18] This suggests a kind of completion. But there is also a moment later on in his poetry, where Thomas seems to question his own motives for this move ever more deeply into Wales. In the curious, glorious poetic autobiography *The Echoes Return Slow*, he muses on this move west, to a landscape embedded deeply in the soul of Wales, from which he could look back across the sea towards the time of his youth. But, he reflects, was there more wisdom to be found in his poetry than in his actions?[19] It seems that the journey to Aberdaron, the 'destination of his own pilgrimage', to a home that might tell him who he was, unexpectedly showed him the limitations of any pilgrimage towards constructing ourselves. And his poetry spoke the wisdom of an emerging and profound move towards accepting himself, reaching beyond any kind of ordinary self-understanding or conscious integration of disparate parts of his character. 'This to do' seems to be an acceptance of that which must be surrendered, with no real hint at what might emerge; an acceptance that to lose your life – even a carefully crafted life – is to find it.

This seems to be another facet of acceptance as Thomas reaches beyond any carefully shaped picture of who he thinks he is, or any understanding of what might have happened to shape him. He does not present himself as victim or victor in his life, bemoan his own sins or folly, or share a self-image that might appeal to his vanity (as far as we can tell). This is simply a time of recognizing that he must enter a new *level* of acceptance, which requires plunging into the depths

> ... to search for the door
> To myself in dumbness and blindness
> And uproar of scared blood
> At the eardrums.

The only thing required for this next step is courage, a costly quality, to be bought with the 'poor / Purse of my body', and paid for with 'the coins of [his] breath'. 'This to do' suggests the riskiness of this kind of acceptance, and with its language of immersion into a depth where there are 'no signposts' but the 'bones of the dead / Conger', there is a sense of profound disorientation, necessary before new life might emerge. Here are the depths of the sea at their most haunting, most frightening: every image takes us further into the deepest places in the ocean, where there are creatures of the deep; where the light, the 'pale / Phosphorous', is light that is refracted in darkness, and where there are 'slow corpses' moving in the depths: the shades, perhaps, of identities no longer needed. This appears to be an acceptance of self so profound that it involves a death; a death of the part of himself that has been constructed, carefully, over many years as priest and poet, for a deeper acceptance to emerge.

Because 'This to do', with its watery imagery, its loss of control, its willing surrender of self, seems to be a poem of baptism at its most risky, with all the potential for drowning and for being overwhelmed. It is a poem of being called into a new depth of identity that requires searing honesty, courage, risk and hope, and, as so often with Thomas's poetry, the way in which the language of a poem is put together deepens its tone and mood. From the urgency of the beginning in which Thomas imagines plunging determinedly into the sea of his interior world, we are taken with him, through an extended metaphor, into a frightening watery quest to 'search for the door / To myself'. The direct but always dreamlike quality of the poem with the initial, arresting declaration, followed by the imagery of diving, has the effect of taking us on the journey that Thomas has said that he must travel, with all the attendant fear, darkness and breathlessness. In 'This to do', we accompany him into the interior, find ourselves in the company of the 'slow corpses', and see the world through the watery luminescence of the 'pale / Phosphorous'.

The strangeness of this poem, its directness and depth, may be shocking, and we may even be hard pressed to find a clear reference to God in among the swaying tendrils in the water. But the whole of 'This to do' has the baptismal quality of the liminal moment; that moment of gift or decision, when what we have known may give way to a kind of death, and this may in turn bring new life and new understanding, even though this has not yet happened and we have not seen it. This is an Advent acceptance of ourselves. It is an acceptance that our life, for all our careful planning and shaping, is wrapped up in the coming Christ. An acceptance that losing our life may be the finding of it.

> I have this that I must do
> One day.

Week 2 – Accepting

Day 3

The Moor

It was like a church to me.
I entered it on soft foot,
Breath held like a cap in the hand.
It was quiet.
What God was there made himself felt,
Not listened to, in clean colours
That brought a moistening of the eye,
In movement of the wind over grass.

There were no prayers said. But stillness
Of the heart's passions – that was praise
Enough; and the mind's cession
Of its kingdom. I walked on,
Simple and poor, while the air crumbled
And broke on me generously as bread.

The Moor

The difference in tone between yesterday's and today's poems could not be greater. After the struggle of 'Amen', and the profound challenge of 'This to do', the poem 'The Moor' takes us into a new landscape of rich reflection, and a different quality of acceptance.

'The Moor', like 'Amen' and 'This to do', emerged at a time when Thomas was discovering the presence of God in the depths of the world, and moving into a more profoundly realized interiority. This was also written at a time when the

religious language of depth was gaining greater currency gener-
ally; Paul Tillich and John Robinson, for example, whose work
Thomas read, contributed to this new and sometimes shock-
ing language for God. Bishop John Robinson it was who, in
his 1963 book *Honest to God*, challenged the familiar way of
seeing God as 'spiritually and metaphysically "out there"',[20]
and instead used the language of presence and depth: we might
see, he said, that the 'holy is the "depth" of the common'.[21]

John Robinson's ideas were considered revolutionary in
the early 1960s, and still seem fresh and startling now, but
to speak of the 'holy' as the '"depth" of the common' seems
to capture the spirit of the Advent journey as we await God's
presence with us again, and accept the glorious gift of God-
with-us in our earthly life. 'The holy is the "depth" of the
common' in Mary, the God-bearer carrying a holy child in the
depth of her body; 'the holy is the "depth" of the common'
in the fluttering heartbeat of the newborn infant, quickening
with miraculous life; 'the holy is the "depth" of the common'
in the byre, sufficient for the first bed of God, come among us
as a child. And our acceptance of our world as a place of gift,
of holiness as the 'depth' of the common is part of our Advent
journey; acceptance that awaiting God's presence does not
mean preparing ourselves for another reality than our own,
but for discovering our world as the home of God, and our-
selves as utterly God's creatures, caught up in God's life by our
very existence.

'The Moor' expresses with great simplicity, beauty and
resonance this idea of the holy as the depth of the common. To
read the poem is to be flooded with Thomas's own experience
of meeting God in this place of earth and colour, in which God
is neither heard nor thought about, neither conjured nor seen,
but absorbed and felt as holiness and as presence. The poem
was based on a specific experience of walking the moors, and
some years later he described the moment that gave birth to
this poem:

I'm a nature mystic, and silence and slowness and bareness
have always appealed. And when I was in Montgomeryshire,

rather than the valley in which I lived, I sought out the moor-
land, and as I left the road and walked to the moorland, it
was very similar to entering a church, a quiet church.[22]

'It was like a church to me', the poem begins, and immediately
we are embedded in the holy. In the image of 'Breath held like
a cap in the hand', we experience, with Thomas, the hushed
reverence of the churchgoer who removes their hat in recog-
nition of entering God's home, or goes before God 'cap in
the hand', humbly, in supplication. The carrying of a cap in a
sacred place, then, is an image that carries with it associations
of churchgoing tradition and with emotional response, but
Thomas takes it further. It is *breath* that is 'held like a cap in
the hand', and all at once, we are caught up more deeply with
the sense of wonder and awestruck silence of this experience of
walking on the moorland. We imagine the catching of breath
that comes with love, or with joyful surprise. And the brief,
very brief, next line, deepens our response to this experience,
of having our breath taken away. 'It was quiet.'
    In mood, this ends the first part of the first part of a poem
which is in sonnet form. This profoundly personal experience
of the holiness of the moorland moves from silent reverence,
which is like the 'gathering' in a church service, towards an
exploration of God's presence, this God who makes

> ... himself felt,
> Not listened to, in clean colours
> That brought a moistening of the eye,
> In movement of the wind over grass.

Is the moistening of the eye an emotional response to a God
who quickens the moorland – or a response to revelation and
encounter? Or are tears brought stinging to eyes through the
brightness of 'clean colours', or the wind over the grass? They
may be tears that hold together both holiness and depth; an
entirely natural response to wind and cold, but hinting too at
the impact of God's presence, felt, absorbed, in the glory of the
moorland. This God of the moor is intangible, but cannot but

be experienced within the very physicality of the landscape, and within the answering response of Thomas.

With the word 'grass', the first part of this sonnet ends; we have moved from a church in the first line, to grass at the last; 'the holy' found to be the '"depth" of the common'. When the break between the two sections comes (the volta in a sonnet), there is, not surprisingly given that 'volta' means 'turn', another change of tone. The silence deepens. Thomas reflects on the impact of the holy, ordinary landscape of this moorland which is like a church, where, despite there being 'no prayers said', yet there *is* praise. And there is acceptance. This is no place to continue a habitual churning of heart or dominance of mind. It is no place to pursue the very human urge to *know*, to rationalize, to put in boxes God and world. Desire and intellect are somehow transcended in the 'stillness / Of the heart's passions', and the 'mind's cession / Of its kingdom'. Thomas surrenders to the immense presence in which he finds himself, and 'walk[s] on' his way, now a participant in a landscape that reveals God, and in which the air becomes the eucharistic host.

Here the moorland both points towards God for Thomas and also reflects the God to which it points, somehow making God present in the sheer physicality of the landscape. And Thomas is called on to surrender and accept, but not as a passive observer who is reminded of God by the beauty of the countryside. He is changed by the revelation, and accepts the falling away of 'the heart's passions' and the respite from the intellect's mastery, to become 'Simple and poor'.

It is at this moment that the air breaks on him, 'generously as bread,' and the body of Christ comes to meet him in the heartbeat of the world. 'The holy is the "depth" of the common.'

Week 2 – Accepting

Day 4

The Bright Field

I have seen the sun break through
to illuminate a small field
for a while, and gone my way
and forgotten it. But that was the pearl
of great price, the one field that had
the treasure in it. I realize now
that I must give all that I have
to possess it. Life is not hurrying

on to a receding future, nor hankering after
an imagined past. It is the turning
aside like Moses to the miracle
of the lit bush, to a brightness
that seemed as transitory as your youth
once, but is the eternity that awaits you.

The Bright Field

'The Bright Field' has become one of Thomas's most well-known poems. It circles around a moment – or moments – of revelation, leading to a kind of acceptance and surrender to God's grace. There is a simplicity to this poem, and a gentle charm, and yet it is also surprising, subtle and gloriously shaped so that the poem's sonnet structure, its language and images all support each other in a form of exquisite beauty.

Fairly unusually for Thomas, this is a poem that is suffused with brightness from the beginning, but less unusually for this nature-loving poet, it is the natural world that provides the breathtaking setting. It was here, in the countryside, on the moorlands, in the sunlight and among all the finery of nature, that Thomas's God spoke to him, whispered, roared and murmured to him most readily. As we saw in 'The Moor', for Thomas, the natural world had a sacramental quality to it, and appeared to him to be 'an outward and visible sign of an inward and spiritual grace',[23] spontaneously mediating God's presence. And so the poem begins with a vision of light pouring on to the Welsh countryside, so that the seer – Thomas – momentarily glimpses a world transfigured. The landscape remains essentially the same, but is transformed in the explosion of light, into a place of divine gift and grace. But then we are immediately faced with something curious and surprising. Even though this explosion of light is the opening, dominant image of the poem, it seems that it is not after all based on a specific moment of epiphany when the world stopped and Thomas reached into the gift of God offered in landscape, light and birdsong. Instead, it appears to have its origins in his memories and reflections on a moment missed: on *not* having been arrested enough by the vision of bright illuminating sunlight to stop him in his tracks.

> I have seen the sun break through
> to illuminate a small field
> for a while, and gone my way
> and forgotten it ...

'Gone my way / and forgotten it', Thomas says, with a note of trailing melancholy – of sadness. As he recalled elsewhere, he has forgotten the moments when he experienced a 'small field lit up by a ray of sunlight' revealing the closeness of 'the heaven we seek'.[24] He has allowed to escape from his grasp the 'sun suddenly strik[ing] through a gap in the clouds and fall[ing] on some field and the trees around'.[25] He had the experiences, but they slipped away, and in 'The Bright Field' we have opened before us both the intense power and the fragility of these memorable, easily lost moments. It is as if the hovering loss and fleeting quality of these moments is as much a part of them as their potential revelation, as their existence at all; to accept *this* is to know more deeply the presence that quickened the landscape for a moment, and quickens it for an eternity, with intense transfiguring brightness.

Typically with R. S. Thomas, the meaning of the poem is shaped and deepened by its movement and the language he uses: allusions to light and fire (the 'miracle / of the lit bush', 'brightness') build on the central image of the bright field. But the reflections and allusions that Thomas weaves through the poem also move the reader beyond this core image. By the end of the poem, it is not the bright field itself that carries the poem's central force and meaning, but that to which 'The Bright Field' points: a glimpse of eternity, of the kingdom of God through a particular place and in a particular moment of time, at the heart of the sunlit field. Immediately after we are told that Thomas has let such moments pass, he introduces the pearl of great price, bringing before us the parable in Matthew's Gospel in which Jesus describes the kingdom of heaven as 'a merchant in search of fine pearls', who sells all he has to possess a 'pearl of great price',[26] and so Thomas transforms the potential moments of stopping in a sunlit field into images of encounter with the kingdom of God; at once costly (he – we – must 'give all' fully to 'possess' it) and also utterly free, to be found at the heart of God's creation, God-with-us in the natural world. And so the poem takes us through a sunlit vision, through epiphany, and loss, and towards reflection and acceptance. And, as in 'The Moor', all is held in the sonnet structure of the poem, pivoting around the volta.

As the first eight lines draw to a close, we hear that:

> ... Life is not hurrying
>
> on to a receding future, nor hankering after
> an imagined past ...

This signals a break. It signals a shift from memory and reflection on the memory, towards a deeper reflection on the meaning of his experiences; a shift from *chronos* to *kairos*; the temporality with which we are daily familiar, to the intersection of time and eternity in the present. And this shift is deepened through the structure of the poem. In breaking the line at 'Life is not hurrying', Thomas emphasizes the movement of the theme. The pause after 'not hurrying', momentarily stops time, but also links with the ideas of the second stanza. Life is not hurrying ...

Once into the final six lines the reflection continues, at first along an unreliable axis of past and future (one is 'receding' and the other 'imagined') before settling on a movement that is neither past nor forward, but 'turning / aside', stepping away from the trajectory of linear time, and towards *kairos*. And in this 'turning aside', 'like Moses' to the burning bush, we see again the bright field-light of the earlier section, but now it as if the field is doubly transfigured by this image with all its overtones of God's revelation in the brightly burning, never-consuming fire of Moses' encounter with God; the sacred at the heart of the ordinary.[27]

In the closing lines of 'The Bright Field', Thomas takes us further into the image of transfiguring light. Its sudden flaring branches into two ideas: the brevity of a human life bound in time, flaring brightly for a while before dying down, and, alongside this, a brightness that is also, he says, 'the eternity that awaits you'. And still the image branches out: in the word 'eternity', Thomas may refer to life beyond death, or that moment that is experienced with such intensity that we are left with a sense of the eternal even in the temporal. The echoes reverberate on, and *kairos* and *chronos* collapse, somehow, into one.

The note on which 'The Bright Field' ends is, again, a curious one, striking as it does a kind of spiritual '*hiraeth*', an intense and wistful longing, born out of separation. But unlike its cultural counterpart, which suggests a nostalgic longing for what might never have been, in 'The Bright Field' this *hiraeth* is a yearning, or a plaintive hope, for what *already* exists – is present – yet all too often missed through failure or inability to acknowledge its presence. Yet in this layered poem of revelation and acceptance, Thomas suggests that more is required than a plaintive hope, a wistful back-glance, a passive awareness of a sunlit landscape, or a vague hope, if God is to be revealed. He suggests that *we* are called to accept that we are living lives caught between the past, with its 'transitory' brightness, and the 'eternity that awaits [us]'. And we are called to accept the invitation to 'turn ... aside' and step out of *chronos* time, to experience the moment of epiphany that hovers at the meeting place of divine revelation and human participation.

We are called to accept the collapsing of time which comes in the season of Advent, and the experience of gift and grace.

Week 2 – Accepting

Day 5

Emerging

Not as in the old days I pray,
God. My life is not what it was.
Yours, too, accepts the presence of
the machine? Once I would have asked
healing. I go now to be doctored,
to drink sinlessly of the blood
of my brother, to lend my flesh
as manuscript of the great poem
of the scalpel. I would have knelt
long, wrestling with you, wearing
you down. Hear my prayer, Lord, hear
  my prayer. As though you were deaf, myriads
of mortals have kept up their shrill
cry, explaining your silence by
their unfitness.
                It begins to appear
this is not what prayer is about.
It is the annihilation of difference,
the consciousness of myself in you,
of you in me; the emerging
from the adolescence of nature
into the adult geometry
of the mind. I begin to recognize
you anew, God of form and number.
There are questions we are the solution
to, others whose echoes we must expand
to contain. Circular as our way
is, it leads not back to that snake-haunted

garden, but onward to the tall city
of glass that is the laboratory of the spirit.

Emerging

How do we pray? Do we share our heartfelt needs with God;
do we ask for what matters most to us? Do we petition and
persist, demand and direct? Do we rest or do we wrangle?
What is the vision of prayer that we carry within us? Do we
share, with the Gospel of St Matthew, the prayer of 'Thy will be
done',[28] or do we carry the psalmist's broken-hearted prayerful
lament? And does our prayer change with life's seasons, or
with circumstance?

'Emerging', the first of two poems that Thomas wrote with
this name,[29] is a poem of prayer changing over the poet's life-
time, a change that seemed to go hand in hand with Thomas's
changing relationship with and understanding of God.
Whether it was prayer that re-shaped his experience of God
or vice versa, in this first 'Emerging' poem we glimpse that life
has changed: Thomas understands and experiences God in a
new way, and prayer is at the very heart of this; it is the ebb
and flow, the language and the hum in the wires that shapes a
whole relationship.

Up to now, prayer has been the river of words and thoughts,
emotions and desires poured out to God: the spoken, the felt
and the thought; but it has now become something different.
'Not as in the old days I pray, / God', Thomas begins, address-
ing God: my life is not what it was. 'Once I would have asked /
healing', he goes on, and like countless praying souls over the
centuries – like all of us – prayer would have been a place of
crying out to be heard, seeking an answering echo, sometimes
only to become a place of self-reproach, in response to God's
apparent silence. We must, we may think, be 'unfit' to be so
ignored in prayer. But,

It begins to appear
this is not what prayer is about.

Prayer and pray-er have been turning on their axis; the one asking healing now recognizes that prayer is not *his* to direct; not an action or a set of words, or a place of bargaining. He now goes 'to be doctored', and with overtones of Holy Communion (drinking 'sinlessly of the blood / of my brother'), expresses the surrender and meeting this sacrament offers; re-shaping us as prayer does, his 'flesh' a 'manuscript of the great poem / of the scalpel'. For the poet, this re-shaping leads towards the realization that prayer is not a series of utterances; it is 'the annihilation of difference', a space or place of union with God. With this, there is the *'emerging'* of a new vision of God; and in this word, dropped quietly into the second half of this poem called 'Emerging', we discover its heart.

There is a prayerful wisdom that emerges. It re-shapes heart and mind, relinquishes the 'shrill cry' and sense of 'unfitness' of the pray-er, abandons the chasm of prayer as something to be argued across, accepts the indwelling of God, and accepts too that our agency is always held, always shaped and contained by a greater wisdom than our own. And in this emerging vision, Thomas sees God from a new vantage point, discovered afresh as 'God of form and number', a mathematical God, whom Thomas explored often from the 1970s onwards. God, who creates, sustains and quickens us, was explored increasingly not only as a 'poet who sang creation', as Thomas described Him, but 'also an intellect with an ultra-mathematical mind, who formed the entire universe in it'.[30] So the poet increasingly explored the possibility that the intricate web of being that underpins our life might be expressed as much through the symmetry and beauty of equations and formulae shaped by the master mathematician, as it could be in musical vibration brought into being by the composer. The mathematics lying at the heart of our existence – discovered, not created by human mathematics – may reveal the glory of the maker as surely as the artist's flashes of vibrant colour point to God's artistry, or the poet's words reflect but do not create the Word, the 'poet who sang creation'.

Thomas calls this emerging vision the 'adult geometry / of the mind', a strange and evocative image, which somehow hints at a maturity of understanding of our place in God's world. We humans, Thomas suggests, are subject to a pattern or network that underlies our existence, rather than being its architects, and as time passes, as we surrender, offer ourselves and open our hearts, we may be drawn more deeply into this understanding. We may recognize that there are divine equations which hold us, and which are not ours to direct. And so prayer becomes an acceptance that we are not the active agents, directing God's actions. While we bring our needs, desires and hopes to God, while we talk with God and share all that we are, the heart of prayer is in our drawing close to the God who prays through and in us. It is in accepting our part in a God-soaked world, becoming evermore drenched in God's life and spirit, and 'expanding' to contain the 'echoes' of questions, rather than answering them.

And as this season of Advent tells us, and 'Emerging' suggests, our life in God is not linear. Our emergence into an 'adult geometry / of the mind' cannot, itself, be achieved through a formula. We wait again in Advent to welcome God-with-us in Christ, we remember God's surrendered entry into our world, and we look forward to an unknown, unnamed time of return. We wait in timeless time, and surrender ourselves to the circularity of our life in God, called to a deepening maturity away from the garden of our innocence, which always bore the 'snake-haunted' seed for maturity, and onward to the 'tall city / of glass'. There are echoes here of the Advent vision of Christ's return and the Holy City, but we are left with the suggestion that this life of ours in the here-and-now, is the crucible of God's action for us, where we are called to engage with our mathematical God, in the transformation of all things, in this 'laboratory of the spirit'. We accept God with us, not only in time, in the Christ child, but in the very substance of our lives. And we are called to surrender a vision that we are the principals in our relationship with God, and accept the 'adult geometry' of a mind dependent on the filigree of equations and formulae that hold and shape our life; not because we have named them, discovered them into being, but because they have always been there, ready to be discovered in the discerning heart.

Week 2 – Accepting

Day 6

The imperatives of the instincts

The imperatives of the instincts
in abeyance, heart and mind
at one in their contemplation
of the ripening apple never

to fall from the topmost branches
of truth's tree. A site for the repair
of promises that were broken, for picking
up pieces of the smashed dream.

It has the freshness of mushrooms,
proof of the whiteness darkness
can bring forth. It is the timeless
place, the unaccommodated

moment; an interval in the performance
of an unheard music. Do not believe
those who have been everywhere
but here. Tell the poor of the world

there is nothing to pay, no distance
to travel; that they are invited
to the marriage of here and now;
that the crystal in which they look,

grey with foreboding as the moon
with earth's shadow, has this
as its far side, turning necessarily towards
us with the reversal of our values.

The imperatives of the instincts

The poem which begins 'The imperatives of the instincts' has some strong similarities with 'The Bright Field'. This is also a heart-stoppingly beautiful poem which encourages us towards accepting the vital, dynamic power of the present moment. But published some years after 'The Bright Field', this poem seems to offer us a more textured examination of what it means to surrender to the moment at hand: to accept God's presence both in the here and now and in the eternal. There is, here, a sense of time-bound timelessness which holds all things, and resists the tendency to reach towards either the past or the future, in a way that can so easily leave us feeling scattered and fragmented.

The poem, which has no title, comes very close to the end of the final section in R. S. Thomas's four-part 1990 collection *Counterpoint*. This is a poetic sequence that explores a kind of spiritual history of humanity, with contrasting ideas and images circling around key moments in the Christian story of redemption. As we read the sequence, we are taken on a journey through the Christian story, and in the final few poems of *Counterpoint*, it seems that Thomas draws us more and more deeply into an acceptance that, at the heart of the paradoxes and glorious untameability of our faith, and in the midst of all that confuses and defies logic, we might find the timeless stillness of God's presence. But this may only be possible, he seems to tell us, as we let go of the drugs of control and dominance, and resist the urge to domesticate the God who constantly bursts the bounds of our understanding. We must, hints Thomas, allow the 'marriage of here and now' to shape us, reach us, touch us, and discover us like an epiphany, even at the very heart of our physical, temporal existence. There are echoes here of the weeks of Advent, as we prepare for God-with-us in the impossibly minute vastness of the heartbeat of the newly born infant.

The careful crafting, the shape and language of 'The imperatives of the instincts', lead us powerfully and gently through the ideas and themes of the poem. The language throughout the six verses is densely allusive and the structure ripples out from a central core, with the poem shaped to move us into the moment of timelessness at its centre: in the gap between verses three and four, and then out again, with a new vision. That the centre of the poem is a space is itself significant and evocative; for Thomas, any spaces and gaps had become places of God's action rather than simply voids, and we are held, very briefly in this space – in

... the unaccommodated

moment; ...

But we do not simply *arrive* here. Throughout the poem, Thomas has been gently nudging us towards it, first describing – or creating – a kind of distance from the usual internal chatter which we so often experience. Beginning with a stark reference to the 'imperatives' of our instincts and impulses, he draws attention to them – and then lets them fall away. With our instincts 'in abeyance', there is the possibility of moving towards a union of heart and mind, contemplating the fruit on 'truth's tree', which, unlike the fruit on the tree of knowledge, remains in place and 'ripens' from being unpicked. Here is a rich and dense image, suggesting at once humility (resisting picking the fruit); a deepening of wisdom (the ripening of the fruit); the inaccessibility (the 'topmost branches') of the most profound truths, and a willingness to allow all that drives us, instinct and intellectual mastery, to fall away. And so we may discover an attentive, contemplative state, which may also be a place of healing, for the 'repair / of promises' and 'picking / up pieces of the smashed dream'.

We have been led from the things that drive us, into a moment of contemplation and a reflection on the potential for healing of such a moment. And from here Thomas leads us to reflect on the *quality* of the timeless moment. It has 'the freshness of mushrooms', sparks of life and light emerging out of the dark earth. This fresh, bright, healing place, free from striving or need, is 'the timeless / place',

... the unaccommodated

moment; an interval in the performance
of an unheard music.

Here is the core of the poem – the 'unaccommodated / moment':
unaccommodated, perhaps, in all kinds of ways. It might be
without the usual content of time; without knowledge, or
memory. Or it might have no place in our usual experience
of time – it is time-out-of-time, an eternal moment, a space,
which can only be experienced within the narrative of life.
Here, this moment hovers between the two middle verses, in
the very centre of the poem, which is a space, 'an interval in the
performance / of an unheard music'.[31] Like a musical interval,
this is a space that is completely vital. Here, in the heart of the
poem, is the heart of the contemplative moment, where instinct
and intellect are quietened and surrendered in a moment of
acceptance.

From here, the mood of the poem changes as Thomas explores
the 'unaccommodated / moment' from another angle. It is as if
he suddenly turns his head to face outwards and address us as
we read, and urges us not to be fooled by those who have not
discovered this surrendered moment, but to seek it ourselves,
and share with 'the poor of the world' the gift available to
them. Though he does not use the words, we might recognize
this 'marriage of here and now' as the kingdom of God, which
is free to enter and is close at hand, if we could only accept it.
It is the place to which all are invited, where instinct and intel-
lect are quietened and surrendered, where the heart opens and
where acquisitiveness of any kind has no place. This is where
we learn what is of least value and where we learn acceptance
of what is of most value.

Like Advent, this poem leaves us 'with the reversal of our
values'. To enter this unaccommodated moment brings us to
the 'far side' of where we habitually look for life, and how we
habitually see and experience life. As in Advent, we are called
here to accept another way of encountering our world, not as
the place of our own action, but as the place of God's action:

in the human heart, in the pain of the 'smashed dream', in the necessary interval and the ripening of wisdom – and in the vastness of an infant's cry.

Week 2 – Acceptance

Day 7

In Context

All my life I tried to believe
in the importance of what Thomas
should say now, do next.
        There was a context
in which I lived; unseen forces
acted upon me, or made their adjustments
in turn. There was a larger pattern
we worked at: they on a big
loom, I with a small needle,
                drawing the thread
through my mind, colouring it
with my own thought.
        Yet a power guided
my hand. If an invisible company
waited to see what I would do,
I in my own way asked for
direction, so we should journey together
a little nearer the accomplishment
of the design.
        Impossible dreamer!
All those years the demolition
of the identity proceeded.
Fast as the cells constituted
themselves, they were replaced. It was not
I who lived, but life rather
that lived me. There was no developing
structure. There were only the changes
in the metabolism of a body

greater than mine, and the dismantling
by the self of a self it
    could not reassemble.

In Context

How, I wonder, do you picture your relationship with God?
How is your life caught up with and shaped by God, and
how do you understand the mystery of God's life woven into
yours? Do you imagine a to-and-fro between us and God – and
where do you place your trust as your life unfolds? 'In Con-
text' asks and explores these questions and, leading us through
self-mocking, assumed control, bargaining, abandonment and
realization, takes us through a story of acceptance. Here, in
a very personal poem, we find recorded the poet's dawning
realization that while we may think we are in control of our
life – that our life is being gently shaped by God, or even that
we have surrendered to God's guidance – the truth is more
radical than this:

                          ... It was not
I who lived, but life rather
that lived me.

To arrive at such a realization may be a lifetime's work and
along the way, we may find ourselves subject to all manner of
illusions.

    Slowly working our way through the poem, lingering over its
moods and images, we may discover anything from a beauti-
fully wrought reflection of our own experience, to a distant
reverberation – a dim echo of what we have thought and felt
about how our life is wrapped up in God. But whether meeting
us in an arresting parallel or a vague impression, its images
are likely to strike some kind of a chord. Reading the opening
lines of 'In Context' may be a bit like looking in a mirror, as
Thomas reflects on his sense of self-importance:

All my life I tried to believe
in the importance of what Thomas
should say now, do next.

In a tone that is slightly sardonic, slightly plaintive, we may
discover our own, sometimes dimly realized sense of needing
to master our lives. But if the poet slightly laughs at himself,
so too is there the suggestion ('I tried to believe') that to take
seriously the importance of saying and doing is no bad thing.
There is a weightiness about this, a validity of intention, but
Thomas's tone tells us that this is not the whole story, and that
he is sharing a vision of the world which has already left him:
'all my life I tried to believe ...'.

It is not surprising, then, that the poem begins and ends with
complementary visions, developing from those opening lines,
towards a different perspective. The determined, committed,
one-foot-in-front-of-another approach of the opening lines
resolves finally into an acceptance that *this* kind of personal
control and agency may be an illusion, and Thomas is called –
we are called – to surrender to a new vision. By the poem's end,
Thomas has walked us carefully and prayerfully through his
grasp of the 'unseen forces' at play in his life, and the adjusting,
guiding power sharing life's trajectory. On the way, the images
shimmer between a vital but humble assessment of God's ways
with him, and a gentle self-mocking of a former view, which
has been both valid and insufficient.

The three sections after the opening lines lay out this shifting
landscape, and again the language and images are supported
by the poetic structure to bring meaning to the whole. Thomas
breaks from his earlier vision of believing in the 'importance' of
doing and saying, with an echoing break in the line structure,
as we are jolted into an understanding – *his* understanding –
that

There was a context
in which I lived ...

There was always, he says, a greater shaping in which our
own actions take on a new perspective. This greater shaping

has brought unbidden adjustments, fashioning the warp and woof of life in a more textured and complex figure than the Thomas believing in his 'importance' might have conceived. But the experience he describes is still one of near mutuality, or cooperation. His 'small needle' has worked alongside the 'big / loom', and his own mind has been the place where life's threads have been expressed in his own way, his own 'colouring'.

'Yet', he says, in another break in line and mood, even *this* vision of near-mutuality is inadequate. 'A power guided / my hand'. Beyond the 'invisible company', with overtones of the angelic hosts, waiting on him 'to see what [he] would do', while he 'asked for / direction', there was something, some*one*, present and guiding,

> ... so we should journey together
> a little nearer the accomplishment
> of the design.

By now we have somehow been taken beyond 'the importance' of what Thomas was doing and saying; beyond the understanding of the tapestry shared by needle and loom; beyond even the 'journeying together' of the poet and the invisible company. Thomas has been leading *us*, as he has been led, to the acceptance of a radically new and different vision of God's guidance. In the next break in the poem, the gears shift again. The images of mutuality and bargaining in life's journey are challenged, and the vision of life as progression is shaken. 'Impossible dreamer!' declares Thomas. It is too easy, he suggests, to see our lives as marching forwards in conjunction with the God who shapes and guides us, or as an incremental building, based on negotiation and bargaining with God. Thomas now sees that in all of life's twists and turns, in his growing, questioning and self-shaping,

> ... It was not
> I who lived, but life rather
> that lived me.

The fantasy of being the architect of his own life has fallen away in the realization that the very depths of his being are always being shaped by the God who quickens. Thomas's vision finally becomes a tumbling and twisting of words (demolition, proceeded, constituted, replaced), poetically unpicking the fantasy of creating our lives according to our own power, and taking us through the roller coaster of our cells' replacement. This is not within our gift to manage or control: this is the force of life that quickens us; it is the power of God's spirit, coursing through our veins; it is the call of God shaping our lives.

If, in reading 'In Context', we have seen reflected how we have understood our relationship with God; if we have heard an echo of seeking guidance, and of knowing ourselves shaped and coloured by a pattern greater than our own, then there is validity in this. But Thomas reminds us how easy it is to tip into becoming the 'impossible dreamers' who believe that we are the main agents of our life, and have forgotten how to sniff the air for the scent of God-with-us in ways we barely imagine.

On this Advent journey, we are in good company in the call to surrender and accept that life is ours and not ours. It is not ours to bargain with and not ours to control; but it *is* ours to live, as grace and gift.

Mary said, 'Here am I, the servant of the Lord; let it be with me according to your word.' (Luke 1.38)

                                        ... It was not
I who lived, but life rather
that lived me.

WEEK 3

Journeying

So shall my word be that goes out from my mouth; it shall not return to me empty, but it shall accomplish that which I purpose, and succeed in the thing for which I sent it. (Isaiah 55.11)

Week 3 – Journeying

Day 1

Wrong?

Where is that place apart
you summon us to? Noisily
we seek it and have no time
to stay. Stars are distant;
is it more distant still,
out in the dark in the shadow
of thought itself? No wonder
it recedes when we calculate
its proximity in light years.

Maybe we were mistaken
at the beginning or took later
a wrong turning. In curved space
one can travel for ever and not recognize
one's arrivals. I feel rather
you are at our shoulder, whispering
of the still pool we could sit down
by; of the tree of quietness
that is at hand; cautioning us
to prepare not for the breathless journeys
into confusion, but for the stepping
aside through the invisible
veil that is about us into a state
not place of innocence and delight.

Wrong?

As we travel deeper into Advent, we turn our attention to the theme of journeying, to explore motifs both human and divine which take us further along the road towards God-with-us at Christmas. For Thomas, journeying included travel but also moments of stepping aside from the main path to a small side road; it included detours and moments of epiphany and surprise. And it included God's journeying *in* the Word made flesh, and as the 'fast God', forever before us, drawing us on.

The poem 'Wrong?', with its reflection on the experience of 'stepping / aside' from the 'breathless journeys' on which we might embark, recalls the 'turning aside' towards the 'lit bush' which Thomas had, many years before, explored in 'The Bright Field'. But this poem does not focus solely on the 'bright field' moment; it also focuses on the stillness and movement of our relationship with God, as we are forever called into God's presence and forever called to travel, to journey on with the God who eternally draws us. And as always with Thomas, the language and structure enhance the themes being explored. The language of presence ('at our shoulder', 'at hand') hints at God close by, draws us into the subtlety of everyday encounters with a God who is to be found in the heart of the ordinary. But there is too the language of space, distance and darkness, which conjures an ever-receding absence, drawing us on as we travel.

That 'Wrong?' begins with a question, even in its title, alerts us that this will be a poem of questions, or surmising, of challenge. 'Have we been wrong?' we seem to be asked straight away, and so begins a poetic journey in which Thomas asks questions about where we find – or *think* we find – God in the world, and how we respond to God's seeming distance and immediacy. Are we called to travel *towards* the God who draws us? he asks, or rather to discover God's proximity? And then, gradually, gradually, as we read, and weave our way through themes of journeying and stillness, Thomas moves us towards a vision of God revealed in the depths of our world, confounding our tendency to push God out into the stars, far from us rather than near. We are moved from outer to inner; from distant space to interior thought; from clamour to quietness and from busy-ness to receptivity.

'Where is that place apart / you summon us to?' Thomas begins, hinting that where God is to be sought and found within this God-created universe is a matter of 'place'. It is as if our God, whom we seek 'noisily', bustling around with 'no time / to stay' is somehow an object in our world, who is to be found somewhere 'out there', though the more we look, the further this place 'recedes'. And yet, Thomas says, we are 'summoned' to this 'place apart', which is 'distant': a twice-used long, sharp-sounding word, with an emphasis to it that underlines the distance to be travelled.

But if we fast-forward towards the end of the poem, we find that the 'place' of the poem's beginning has become balanced, in the final lines, with 'a state / not place of innocence and delight'. This suggests just how far the poem travels, from the idea of reaching our God in a 'place' that is *out there*, towards the idea, finally, that God is not to be found in a 'place' so much as a condition, or 'state', at the heart of our experience of the world. This comes at the end of the second, longer part of the poem, which, in sharp contrast with the first few lines, explores the single-word title. Have we been looking in the wrong place for God, Thomas seems to ask, and have we been looking in the wrong *way*? Perhaps the 'place apart' is not as we imagined. And have we *always* been looking in the wrong place, or has humanity – have *we* – somehow become lost? In aiming for the 'place apart', seeking God 'out there', we have hurled ourselves outwards, but 'curved space' simply returns us to where we started from. With 'curved space', Thomas circles us around as we read, pulling us back closer to home, and towards a sense of the immanent, intimate God who is not spatially distant, but 'at our shoulder, whispering / of the still pool'. This move from the transcendent God to the immanent takes place within a few lines of the second part of the poem. The short, simple and sharp sounds of the first part of the poem have now given way to the softer, gentler cadences of the second, weaving together to form a picture of the closeness of God. The lines elongate, the sounds of the words feel less staccato, the sibilants softer, and the phrasing more meditative and less hurried. 'I feel rather', says Thomas to God in a sentence lasting over ten lines, 'you are at our shoulder, whispering / of the still pool we could sit down / by'. Ours is not to be a 'breathless journey / into confusion', but a 'stepping / aside' into the 'state / not place' of communion with God.

There is no urgent travelling here. It is as if Thomas is taking us on a poetic journey through curved space, to bring us back to our 'arrivals'. The move is away from frenzied activity, and from seeking God 'noisily', towards receptivity; listening to the hints of the whispering God who speaks in the natural world. And finally, we are brought to the response, which is one of 'stepping / aside', which brings with it a change of direction and perception. This journey takes us 'through the invisible / veil', bringing us a new awareness of the ordinary; an added dimension to the world, so that a 'state' is discovered in the here and now, rather than another 'place' sought, as at the beginning.

There is something about this stepping aside in the here-and-now, into a state of attentive receptivity, which is characteristic of the season of Advent. And this is not stepping aside for a moment only, but stepping aside into a 'state' which takes us through the whole season's journeying, invited as we are to look forward in anticipation, and discover the glory of God's interruption into our human life, in the vulnerability of the Christ child.

We are called to journey and to 'recognize [our] arrivals', at the 'still pool' and the 'tree of quietness'. We are called to step through the invisible veil and discover ourselves on the journey to Bethlehem even as we live our ordinary lives.

Week 3 – Journeying

Day 2

Migrants

He is that great void
we must enter, calling
to one another on our way
in the direction from which
he blows. What matter
if we should never arrive
to breed or to winter
in the climate of our conception?

Enough we have been given wings
and a needle in the mind
to respond to his bleak north.
There are times even at the Pole
when he, too, pauses in his withdrawal,
so that it is light there all night long.

Migrants

Thomas was a bird watcher. Birds swooped and soared through his life. Birds wove through poetry and prose, enticed him away from Wales,[32] were part of the rhythm and shape of time, and coloured his landscape. In 'A Year in Llŷn',[33] a brief, idiosyncratic record of a single year, Thomas writes admiringly about eagle-eyed ornithologists, describes how to begin bird watching, and flips through the pages of *The British Book of Birds* to share the birds which punctuated his year: seagulls, sparrowhawks, greenshanks, treecreepers, owls, skylarks, chiffchaffs, whimbrels, cuckoos. All fill the Welsh air; all move across the horizon, along with the rarer roseate terns, merlins and golden orioles.

And then there are the bird migrants, flying for thousands of miles to breed, and thousands of miles to stay warm, criss-crossing the world and alighting for a season on Welsh soil. Appearing as a trickle in March, a flood in April, and abating again by June, warblers, Hungarian rose-coloured starlings and North American phalaropes all appear, and make their temporary homes. And then, in August, new migrations begin, with sea and sandwich terns preparing to travel away from Wales in cacophonous, flocking preparation, followed by the autumnal journey of wild geese, all instinctively following food, sustenance and warmer air to winter away from the gusting icy winds of the Atlantic.

Those setting out on their migrations do so instinctively, responding to the deeply embedded and unquenchable quest for nourishment and life. They share journeys which are perilous and costly but to stay put would be to perish. To stay put would be to ignore every natural signal to set out and enter the aching space which summons them to begin; to risk, to dare to survive and thrive. The call to the birds to set out instinctively on a journey with an uncertain ending is paradoxically their only hope for life. Little surprise that they inspired a picture of other perilous, life-giving journeys, both closer to home and even bolder in scope than the glorious migratory birds.

The call in Thomas's 'Migrants'[34] is to set out instinctively on a journey that is uncertain, and that is also the call to life. It is the call to a journey that draws us, inexorably, into a space opening up ahead and summoning the traveller to set out onwards towards our origins, our source and our sustainer. Like migrant birds, Thomas suggests, there is within *us* something that naturally and yearningly orientates us towards the God who directs our travels: the God who is everywhere in the poem, but who is curiously named not as a presence but, in the opening line, as a 'great void / we must enter'. Somehow compelling us to embark on the journey, this 'void' has the feel less of vacant space than of the air that we breathe; it is our very atmosphere, filled with currents and gusts, pressures and eddies, lifting us and carrying us if we are prepared to venture out and be caught in the squalls and zephyrs of the journey. God shows us the way with His breath, not by blowing us *towards* our destination, but curiously, by summoning us 'in the direction from which / he blows'. There is no forcing here, but an invitation to travel on, reached and held by the presence of the breath – the Spirit of God – like the air currents that carry migratory birds.

Curiously, like God in this poem, the birds are never named. But the atmosphere of 'Migrants' is so richly drawn, that as we read, we are steeped in their presence as surely as we are steeped in the presence of God. Strangely, we become these travelling birds, launching ourselves into the atmosphere, called to journey on to a landmark beyond the ocean, uncertain of arrival, and even heading towards the Pole. We may find ourselves caught up in the riskiness of this, 'calling / to one another' through the bleak wintry air. And like the birds, we may never reach our destination. But, asks Thomas, does this matter?

> ... What matter
> if we should never arrive
> to breed or to winter
> in the climate of our conception?

Following the impulse to journey into the summoning breath of God, he suggests, is the most important thing, more important even than 'winter[ing] / in the climate of our conception'. This curious phrase, so plaintive and full of yearning, might hint at the myriad desires and motivations which we follow as we journey on, and even our expectations of the God who calls us. Does wintering in the 'climate of our conception' suggest finding refuge in a utopia from which we have been expelled? Is it an unattainable return to the garden of our spiritual origin? Is it to desire a rest – or to expect that we shall be given a rest – from life's vagaries, which leads us endlessly away from our imagined paradise of the mind? Perhaps there is a hint that our traveller's impulse is to pursue a destination beyond this life; to the place from which we set out, and to which we return.

Thomas, of course, gives us no answer. We are not told that all shall be well on our travels, simply that it is 'enough' to have been gifted with our wings for flight and our unerring instinct to 'respond to his bleak north' which is *our* true north. There is no easy spiritual sentimentality here; no rosy glow in our travelling. Following our true north is to accept that our most profound journey is in the slipstream of God, through the light and shade of life; through joy and bleakness, at once buoyed along and buffeted, travelling through life's rigours rather than towards a fantasy ending.

And yet, whereas so often the end of an R. S. Thomas poem is a painful sting in the tail, in 'Migrants' we are shown a glimpse more of light than 'bleak north'. 'There are times even at the Pole', says Thomas, even in the deepest austerity and farthest reaches of the journey, that God

> ... pauses in his withdrawal,
> so that it is light there all night long.

It is as if God looks over His shoulder, beckoning the traveller, who in the darkest of moments is offered illumination. And so, we are drawn on and encouraged again to continue our migrations.

We may be reminded of this in the season of travelling and arriving; of birth and new life. The call is not to resist the natural urge to travel towards God, but to risk the journey. The call is to travel faithfully, hopefully, inevitably. There will be light and there will be shade on the journey, gusts and squalls, and the ending may look nothing like we expected, but 'we have been given wings / and a needle in the mind'. We have been given the gift of following; and that is the journey.

Week 3 – Journeying

Day 3

Pilgrimages

There is an island there is no going
to but in a small boat the way
the saints went, travelling the gallery
of the frightened faces of
the long-drowned, munching the gravel
of its beaches. So I have gone
up the salt lane to the building
with the stone altar and the candles
gone out, and kneeled and lifted
my eyes to the furious gargoyle
of the owl that is like a god
gone small and resentful. There
is no body in the stained window
of the sky now. Am I too late?
Were they too late also, those
first pilgrims? He is such a fast
God, always before us and
leaving as we arrive.
           There are those here
not given to prayer, whose office
is the blank sea that they say daily.
What they listen to is not
hymns but the slow chemistry of the soil
that turns saints' bones to dust,
dust to an irritant of the nostril.

There is no time on this island.
The swinging pendulum of the tide

has no clock; the events
are dateless. These people are not
late or soon; they are just
here with only the one question
to ask, which life answers
by being in them. It is I
who ask. Was the pilgrimage
I made to come to my own
self, to learn that in times
like these and for one like me
God will never be plain and
out there, but dark rather and
inexplicable, as though he were in here?

Pilgrimages

Bardsey Island, Ynys Enlli, rises from the Atlantic, off the tip of the Lleyn Peninsula. Inhabited probably for thousands of years, and a place of pilgrimage for many centuries, the island sits at the end of the North Wales Pilgrim's Way, which runs from the north-east of Wales near the Wirral, along the shoulder and arm, to beyond the fingertip of the Peninsula.[35] This place, often called the burial place of twenty thousand saints, saturated with the lives and prayers of early and medieval Christians as well as modern pilgrims, is still reached by 'a small boat the way / the saints went'. And it still calls the traveller to risk the Atlantic swell to reach the haven of the island.

Finding a 'risky haven' may be a paradox of any pilgrimage or sacred travelling, and Thomas's 'Pilgrimages' rumbles with the paradox of journeying to an island sanctuary along a route that brings danger and asks courage of the traveller. It tells of a destination completely rooted in time and place and tradition, and we are invited into the same journey. But 'Pilgrimages' reminds us of other journeys too – so we as fellow pilgrim travellers might feel ourselves called onwards to further journeys. Is a pilgrimage to this island, then, or any pilgrimage, a place to which we travel – a destination – a staging post, or a picture of all our travelling? Thomas's 'Pilgrimages' hints at all of these.

The first few lines of his poem draw us into the tussling, tumbling world of ancient pilgrimage in raw conditions. Direct, almost rough-hewn language, with a density and intensity of feeling, brings before us endless saints, caught in awe and fear and dedicated journeying to their sacred destinations. To travel to this island is to travel

> ... the gallery
> of the frightened faces of
> the long-drowned, munching the gravel
> of its beaches.

Here we find ourselves among long-gone pilgrims, lodged in the imagination and the reality of Welsh pilgrimage, in the company of St Cadfan and other Celtic saints, travellers who were touched by far-off Egyptian and Syrian communities.[36] We find ourselves in the company of Augustinian monks who found a sanctuary on Bardsey, and the faithful who travelled to Ynys Enlli instead of Rome. And we find ourselves among the lost and the scared, who have trodden the path before us, whose 'frightened faces' conjure up the dangers of this short crossing and the holy awe that can fill a pilgrim's heart on the journey of encountering God. And so innumerable pilgrims have landed on the island, 'munching the gravel / of its beaches'. To linger over this phrase is to discover the richness of Thomas's language and its power to reach heart and mind; in this echo of Lamentations (3.16), we might hear the tread of feet on gravelled shore, or sense the difficult ruminations of the traveller as they journey with God, chewing over this place of encounter. Or we might imagine a pilgrim face-down on the beach, floored by the humility of attending to this sacred, thin place, giving thanks after a wintry, life-threatened crossing.

And then, moving from the sweep of history, we find ourselves alongside a single pilgrim. Thomas finds himself on the island, taking the same route as the pilgrims, 'up the salt lane to the building / with the stone altar' to a destination where God is both found and lost. This has been a place of encounter for centuries; a place for which pilgrims have yearned, for which they have risked the wintry Atlantic, to which they have been called, but in which God has not been fixed, cannot be fixed, and so appears in some strange sense absent. The candles on the stone altar have 'gone out', and the 'furious gargoyle' has the look of an ossified god, 'gone small and resentful'. Even the 'stained window / of the sky' does not reveal God.

Where has the summoning God gone? Where is the God who calls us to journey on as pilgrims? 'Am I too late?' Thomas asks of this absent God, and were those earlier pilgrims also too late for 'such a fast / God', forever pre-empting us in our journeying, and forever departing just as we believe we can fix Him in stained glass, flame, sculpture and altar. Our destinations are never complete, Thomas seems to be saying; to believe we have arrived and to expect to find God rooted in the ways familiar to us is to clutch at the air that stirs as God goes ahead of us, discomfiting us even when we seek sanctuary; drawing us on in new pilgrimages to discover Him afresh.

And then, as so often with Thomas, there is a break in the poem that moves us towards another mood and invites us into a new perspective. 'There are those', he says, who attend to this place of pilgrimage differently; not questing, but *attending*. Suppose, he implies, we too were to attend to our life's pilgrimage differently? Suppose we, even on our Advent journey, were to stop in our tracks and pay attention to the 'slow chemistry of the soil'? Suppose the God whom we can never outpace or catch as we hurry onwards is to be found not in our anxious searching but in the very matter of the earth: in water and dust, and in the very air that we breathe – 'an irritant of the nostril'? Here is a hint of what lies at the heart of the Advent journey: we are travelling towards God, but this is not some absent, distant, far-off 'God up there'. Instead, this is God coming to meet us in our humanity and in God's humanity: God *incarnate*, born into human life and *embodied* in the matter of this world, in cells and flesh and air, catching up our physical world in God's actions. The 'fast God', then, may not be found by catching

Him in a snare before His next departures, but by apprehending the world in a new way; not chasing the 'fast God' who will always outstrip us, but attending to the 'slow chemistry of the soil', and bringing a different lens to bear upon our world, requiring of us a 'deeper immersion in existence'.[37]

And suddenly, the poetic gears change. In this ancient place, which sweeps through the ages, which cannot hold the 'fast God', and where the crumbled earth slowly returns human bone to dust and dust to breath, time ceases to exist: the 'swinging pendulum of the tide / has no clock; the events / are dateless'. The question is no longer speed of journeying along some temporal axis, or even stopping to attend to God-with-us in dust and earth, but dropping down into the depths of the self. Is this, after all, our pilgrimage, asks Thomas: towards the discovery that God-*with*-us is God-*in*-us, in the complexity and messiness of our lives, and in the dimness and mystery of the interior landscape? Our pilgrimage to God, suggests Thomas, takes us inexorably on a journey within, to confront the raw, the unformed, the hopeful, the faithful and the doubting self, who reaches out to God and travels the Advent journey, waiting expectantly to encounter the God who has borne and shaped us.

> ... Was the pilgrimage
> I made to come to my own
> self, to learn that in times
> like these and for one like me
> God will never be plain and
> out there, but dark rather and
> inexplicable, as though he were in here?

Week 3 – Journeying

Day 4

Evening

The archer with time
as his arrow – has he broken
his strings that the rainbow
is so quiet over our village?

Let us stand, then, in the interval
of our wounding, till the silence
turn golden and love is
a moment eternally overflowing.

Evening

'Evening' is an unusual addition during this week of Advent when we focus on journeying. Unusual because there is a stillness about this brief, brief poem. There is a lack of clamour, a lack of movement and direction of travel. It is, though, this very stillness which fits the poem snugly in the middle of this week, calling us to stop for a moment on our journeying, as if we and the poet were able to share a moment of surrendered peace and stillness at the heart of life's inexorable flow and our walk through Advent towards Christmas.

There is too a poignancy about 'Evening'. As we read it and linger over its images, its precisely chosen words and phrases, the stillness we discover may seem both temporal and eternal. This is a stillness that lasts for just the momentary span of our reading, but which also conjures up the stillness of a whole evening in the passage of time. And we are beckoned further into a stillness of the heart which expands beyond a moment, or an evening, inviting us to participate in an eternal stillness which nestles in the soul.

Thomas begins and ends his poem with these different perceptions of time. At first the 'archer with time / as his arrow', describes a line drawn at speed, with time travelling its hurried path until it finds its mark; the meaning is not 'in the waiting' but in reaching its destination. By the end of the poem, however, this sharply delineated trajectory of time has become 'a moment eternally overflowing'. We might want to ask what has happened in this brief, profoundly moving poem, to change this mood so completely; but as ever with Thomas, any attempt completely to explain one of his poems would be inadequate. We can, though, explore its images and their resonances, allow them to speak to us, and allow our own impressionistic pictures to take shape, so that even this briefest of poems can enrich the Advent journey. And we can also reflect a little on how this great poet changes the mood so profoundly in this brief, devotional poem, that we are moved to a new sense of God in stillness and surrender.

'Evening' reads as if it is a response to a moment of epiphany – a revelation of God's presence in the world – which has caused Thomas to stop and experience the complete stillness of this time-out-of-time. Something has happened in the midst of ordinary life which arrests his attention, causes him to perceive the world around him in a new way, and demands a response. And the response itself, as well as the event to which he is responding, somehow ushers in an experience of sacred time; an eternal present. As a rainbow hovers over the village, time appears to have been suspended. The night is so still that Thomas asks if the archer with 'time as his arrow' has broken his strings; has found himself unable to shoot the arrow that will allow time to continue on its trajectory. And so, timelessness descends on (or emerges out of) the village: 'our' village. This 'possessive' has a powerful impact, transforming the poem from something going on 'out there', to something going on within us and around us. This is *our* village we hear at the end of the first verse, and we are invited by Thomas, at the beginning of the second verse, to linger a while in it: 'Let *us* stand, then'.

But these possessives do more; they wrap themselves around the very centre of the poem, around its heart which, as in 'The imperatives of the instincts', is to be found in a space between two verses. Here, in this gently held space between 'our village' and 'Let us stand', the 'interval' is amplified somehow, and we are drawn into the scene. And so we may share with Thomas a meditative experience – almost a reverie – of time arrested, standing still, and shifting from its linear, focused journey. But this moment out of time is not a paradise without pain. It is 'the interval / of our wounding'. This sounds like some strange intermission in a play; an interval between two acts in which we re-orientate ourselves. But this is an intermission or interval which offers momentary freedom from 'our wounding'. What is this wounding? Is this simply the wounding of which human life consists? And is the still space a moment of relief from wounding, or an opportunity simply to focus on what 'is'? Whatever this interval is, in this quiet gap – this temporal space – a moment of epiphany may take place: the silence ripens and 'turn[s] golden' and becomes not simply a place in which love may be accessed, but it *is* love: 'love is / a moment eternally overflowing'.

And so somehow, we may find ourselves in a transfigured world, in which usual perceptions of time and place have been disrupted by the sudden experience of a moment out of time, and the experience of stillness. This interruption in the flow of time is a moment of love and grace, which perhaps feels uncharacteristic of Thomas. But then we might realize that while the context and overwhelming experience held within the poem suggests love, as usual, Thomas does not shy away from hinting at human pain, even in the glorious stillness of a village evening: we are, after all, standing in 'the interval / of our wounding'.

But perhaps what is most striking about 'Evening', a brief poem, but as richly textured as many of his longer ones, is that it appears to be written from *within* the heart of an experience. This is different from both 'The Bright Field', which reflects on a missed opportunity, and another of our journeying poems, 'Wrong?' which seems to reflect experiences known and past. And so 'Evening' brings us up short; it stops us in the tracks of our journeying and beckons us to be still for a moment. Just for a moment.

Week 3 – Journeying

Day 5

I know him

I know him.
He is the almost anonymous,
the one with the near perfect
alibi, the face over us that lacks
nothing but an expression.
He is the shape in the mist
on the mountain we would ascend
disintegrating as we compose it.

He can outpace us
in our pursuit, outdistancing
time only to disappear
in a black hole. He acknowledges
our relationship in the modes of thought
repudiating, when we would embody
thought in language, a syntactical
compulsion to incorporate
him in the second person.

I know him

'I know him' is one of Thomas's brief, apparently simple, deeply textured and baffling poems. If the journey we go in when reading it were drawn, it might look like a labyrinth.

The language is straightforward, easy and direct, but so too is it convoluted, taking us in twists and turns through a flurry of ideas and allusions which appear, and then turn back on themselves. If we were to follow the labyrinth of 'I know him', we would be taken along a path that circles around and doubles back, taking us closer and closer towards some kind of centre. But unlike in a labyrinth, we would not find ourself at an end point – some settled destination of the heart where we find God – because the God towards whom we travel in 'I know him' would ultimately disappear like a wisp. And yet in disappearing, this God might become more tantalizingly present, filling all our thoughts and desires as we are drawn on in the journey.

The invitation, then, is to read 'I know him' once and once again. The invitation is to allow the language and its meanings to seep in and to allow the journey to begin; to follow the labyrinth as we are led towards God, and to continue all the twists and turns of the journey. And on the way, we shall encounter a riot of ideas and baffling paradoxes in curiously negative language, which is so tumultuous, so crackling in its oppositions, that thought is stretched and ideas pushed to the limit. And when *this* happens – when familiar language is suddenly subverted, something new can break through; because the God who draws us on cannot be described in flat language, but *may* be glimpsed in oppositions which leave us breathless and inarticulate.

The poem begins, simply, with 'I know him', but immediately, in the following lines, this turns around as we realize that we have to re-understand these words. Does Thomas *actually* know God? Perhaps he is being slightly arch, ironic, knowing that we can never fully know God. Or perhaps what he knows is God's ways with us, rather than God Himself.

And so the journey begins, pointing us towards familiar ideas in unfamiliar ways, which paint a perplexing picture of a God whom we know and don't know; whom we draw close to only to discover that He has gone; who evades our grasp just as we think our fingers are closing around Him. In 'I know him', God so nearly appears time and time again; so nearly comes before us but never quite shows His face. He is the 'almost anonymous', we hear, the one who is unknowable, but not quite; unnamed but not quite; unremarkable but not quite. The 'near perfect / alibi' explains His absence, but not quite, and hints inevitably at both elusiveness and inevitable presence. His face 'over us that lacks / nothing but an expression', is at once complete and invisible; watchful but avoiding our gaze. As mountain mist, He takes a shape which 'we compose', but which then disappears. Perhaps Thomas is hinting that the God who surrounds us and takes shape before us, 'disintegrates' because this is an image of our own making – our composition. Or perhaps God reaches us in a way we can apprehend, on a journey we know, but still is never fully resolved before us.

In the first part of the poem, then, we circle around the labyrinth, finding ourselves confronted by the God who compels us to move ever closer to the centre, yet remains ungraspable. We are in a world saturated by the immanent God who nevertheless eludes us, and so we find ourselves deep in the ancient tradition of 'unsaying',[38] a way of speaking about God, but also saying the opposite. With 'unsaying', we are called never to rest in any definition of God, but always to travel onwards, full of yearning, to further meanings.

And then the ground shifts as the journey takes us further along the labyrinthine path towards the outer reaches of the cosmos, only to turn back again into the intimacy of humanity, in our language and thought. Like a wild animal, or a shooting star, this ungraspable God runs ahead of us 'in our pursuit'; we follow, full pelt, but God is too fast not only for us, but for time itself, 'only to disappear in a black hole'. Thomas, fascinated by the cosmos, by God as the architect of the stars, now plays with space and time. And as this poem came out just two years after Stephen Hawking wrote *A Brief History of Time*, it is possible that his reference to black holes draws on this modern masterpiece, because how Hawking describes the black hole is tantalizingly close to how Thomas talks about God who is perpetually out of reach and yet only a hair's breadth away. To fall into a black hole, says Hawking, is to 'reach the region of infinite density and the end of time'.[39] And the boundary of the black hole, the 'event horizon', is 'formed by the light rays … hovering forever just on the edge', from which nothing can escape; 'it is a bit like running away from the police and just managing to keep one step ahead but not being able to get clear away!'[40] The black hole, then, takes us through time and beyond time, journeying unfathomable distances, and creating unbreakable proximity; all of time and space, and the ending of time and space, coalesce in this one image.

And then, having been flung into space and beyond time, in the circling and endlessly turning journey of 'I know him', we are returned to the intimacy of thought and expression, again finding ourselves in our very human desire to name and grasp God. And in a final, circuitous image, we discover, embodied in the poem's form and words, what it means to find God beckoning us in our minds, then slipping away as we try to give voice to our thoughts. 'He acknowledges / our relationship in the modes of thought', says Thomas, straightforwardly enough; but we don't stop here. Looping round on to the next line, as if following the contours of an idea, we discover that no sooner does God reach us in thought, but that He 'repudiate[s],

> ... when we would embody
> thought in language, a syntactical
> compulsion to incorporate
> him in the second person.

God rejects our desire to turn thought into language, and pin Him down in a name; and the language Thomas uses to express this is so slippery and elaborate, it is as if the words themselves are tumbling away from us as we read them – embodying the generous elusiveness of God, who refuses our attempts to pin Him down, and so remains alive for us, leading us ever onwards, in yearning pursuit. This is 'speech about God which is a failure of speech', to borrow words from Denys Turner,[41] both declaring the immense presence and transcendence of God, and showing us that nothing we say can be equal to the God for whom we wait at Advent.

The God of 'I know him' recedes but does not disappear. This God draws us on in His slipstream, just as He was drawn into life in Christ at Christmas; just as the shepherds, the Magi and countless others were drawn and are still drawn. Just as we are drawn and say 'yes' to the journey, following through the twists and turns of life. This evasive, ungraspable God of 'I know him' reminds us of the 'now and not yet' of living as Christ's people on our journey again towards His new life, but also of the greater 'not yet' of which we are reminded in Advent: the 'not yet' of waiting for the whole of creation to be freed and restored, in God's kingdom which is both with us, and just over the horizon.

Week 3 – Journeying

Day 6

The Moon in Lleyn

The last quarter of the moon
of Jesus gives way
to the dark; the serpent
digests the egg. Here
on my knees in this stone
church, that is full only
of the silent congregation
of shadows and the sea's
sound, it is easy to believe
Yeats was right. Just as though
choirs had not sung, shells
have swallowed them; the tide laps
at the Bible; the bell fetches
no people to the brittle miracle
of the bread. The sand is waiting
for the running back of the grains
in the wall into its blond
glass. Religion is over, and
what will emerge from the body
of the new moon, no one
can say.
                    But a voice sounds
in my ear: Why so fast,
mortal? These very seas
are baptized. The parish
has a saint's name time cannot
unfrock. In cities that
have outgrown their promise people

are becoming pilgrims
again, if not to this place,
then to the recreation of it
in their own spirits. You must remain
kneeling. Even as this moon
making its way through the earth's
cumbersome shadow, prayer, too,
has its phases.

The Moon in Lleyn

The Lleyn Peninsula, that gunslinger arm reaching out into the Atlantic Ocean, is a place of dramatic skies; of bright moons hovering in raw, inky blackness. Here, in this Precambrian outcrop, it is possible to imagine – to experience – time reaching through thousands of years, but forever hovering in the moment, in the fruit of dextrous human crafting, the movement of the seasons, and the natural reminders of lost ages. It is no surprise that the moon of the Lleyn conjures rich visions of time and eternity. Nor is it a surprise that Thomas's poem 'The Moon in Lleyn' takes us through imaginary and mythic journeys, and calls us towards an understanding that our snapshot view of time, frozen and locked in a moment, can lead us astray from the sweep of God's time. And it is a poem that can return us to the gift of the divine, embodied moment; the gift of the incarnation.

The fourth-quarter moon which hovers over the peninsula is, for Thomas, a reminder of endings and beginnings: of the death of religion and the birth of something new. Kneeling in the emptiness of a stone church, a familiar place for Thomas, he finds it 'easy to believe' that the world is turning around him, the congregations have fled and no one will be summoned any more to the eucharistic heart of faith, 'the brittle miracle / of the bread'. Echoing Yeats' poem 'The Second Coming',[42] this bleak, primal landscape hints at the end of the Christian Era which has borne and shaped us. 'Religion is over', the moon, silence, shadows and windswept darkness seem to say;

the 'tide laps / at the Bible' and the 'last quarter of the moon / of Jesus gives way / to the dark'.

Can it be true, Thomas asks in 'The Moon in Lleyn', that we are on a bleak Yeatsian journey towards a new, unknowable and unfathomable time, as history tumbles on in overlapping aeons? Is the age of Christ ebbing away as the 'serpent digests the egg',[43] and is there some cosmic hatching at hand? And if so,

> what will emerge from the body
> of the new moon, no one
> can say.

'No one can say.' There are questions; faith seems bruised, churchgoers dwindle; what lies ahead is unknown. All is uncertain. And then God speaks.

The line break in the centre of the poem, as usual with Thomas, signals a shift and we find ourselves with a completely different mood and on a completely different journey. Or rather a different narrative, as the second part of the poem interprets the signs of times in a new way and tells us a different story. There is no denial that the lost shadows of congregations might point to an end of an era, but now we are invited into a deeper understanding of this place and God's presence in it. We are invited to see beyond the surface, and to read this pre-Cambrian outcrop of land, over which the fourth-quarter moon hangs, its churches, its history and its present, in a completely different way. This is a place saturated in God's presence, not losing an identity, but forever steeped in the Christ who, unusually for Thomas, is named at the outset of the poem. Even if the faithful no longer flock to a church; even if the tide laps at the Bible and the 'brittle miracle / of the bread' no longer summons the human heart, yet the age of Christ is not over. The apparently departing, but ever-present Christ, lives in the landscape, and at our peril do we read our world as Christ-less.

'Why so fast, mortal?' asks the God who watches how we read our world. Why so fast to declare the end of an age? Why so fast to conclude that Christ has departed because the familiar places in which we find Him have changed? To read a mere snapshot of our changing world as a permanent picture of God's absence would be to fail to see a wider, broader, deeper sweep of God's presence. After all, says God, 'these very seas / are baptized'. Baptizing water, itself baptized, surrounds the ancient land, drenched in God's presence. And the parish 'has a saint's name time cannot / unfrock'. This is no throwaway faith, lost as the times change, but a landscape saturated, quickened and baptized by God's presence. And as the language of the first half of the poem, characterized by loss and ending (silent, shadows, laps, brittle, dark, swallowed, over), gives way to language of sacred presence (baptized, saint, pilgrims, kneeling, spirits, recreation), so we are called to re-understand the presence of God in our world, and to become pilgrims again. If the gyres (cycles and spirals of time) are turning as Yeats suggested, perhaps the journey we are on is not away from Christ, but towards a deeper recognition of God-with-us in Christ, the incarnate one, as the world shouts His presence in rock and sand, in moon and prayer; in our 'own spirits'.

The journey of 'The Moon in Lleyn', then, is not linear, towards a Godless time, but seems to be a cyclic journey towards new and deepening encounters with God. The fourth-quarter moon of Lleyn *is* a moment of transition, but it is also an invitation towards depth and re-encounter, just as Advent, at the very beginning of the Church's annual cycle, is an invitation towards encountering Christ again in the incarnation. We may be called to be pilgrims; we may be called to see into the depth of the places we inhabit; we may be called to slow down and to listen to the God who speaks in unexpected ways. Whatever we are called to do, we are certainly called to 'remain kneeling', and follow prayer's phases as surely as we follow the waxing and waning of the moon.

And as the gyres turn, and the annual cycle of the Church's year finds us again in Advent, we might want to reflect on what, in this cyclic journey of re-encounter, we are revisiting in our own lives. We might want to ask how Christ is coming to us this year, and where we discover Him anew in life. We might want to read the signs around us freshly and discover what in our lives is 'baptized', what we carry within us which cannot be gainsaid, and what is waiting to be born. And we might want to reach into our world and read the signs of God's presence around us.

Reach deeper. We are on no linear journey, but an Advent cycle of new birth, of the never absent, ever returning Christ.

Week 3 – Journeying

Day 7

Llananno

I often call there.
There are no poems in it
for me. But as a gesture
of independence of the speeding
traffic I am a part
of, I stop the car,
turn down the narrow path
to the river, and enter
the church with its clear reflection
beside it.
　　　　　There are few services
now; the screen has nothing
to hide. Face to face
with no intermediary
between me and God, and only the water's
quiet insistence on a time
older than man, I keep my eyes
open and am not dazzled,
so delicately does the light enter
my soul from the serene presence
that waits for me till I come next.

Llananno

As we travel through Advent, we might ask ourselves what kind
of journey are we taking. Are we journeying towards something
or away from something, or simply travelling? Perhaps we

are travelling at our usual pace of life: we might be moving at speed, pell-mell, rushing through the season, from encounter to encounter. Or we might be ambling and lingering on the path, being distracted, enjoying shifts and changes in speed. Whatever the manner of our journeying, we may wonder if we are allowing ourselves a change of pace: allowing moments of stillness to shape our experience of travelling, as much as the movement.

'Llananno' is a poem of both movement and stillness. It is based on the hamlet of Llananno which lies a few miles from Llandridod Wells, just off the A483. Its church, dedicated to the mysterious St Anno, about whom little is known,[44] is a Victorian rebuilding of a far older place of worship, dating from at least the Middle Ages, and possibly Celtic times. A simple and modest building from the outside, this is the church of Thomas's 'Llananno', unremarkable enough to have 'no poems in it' for Thomas. And yet this is, for him, a place of pilgrimage, where he 'often call[s]': both destination and punctuation on a longer journey. A stopping point, a junction, and a meeting place: huddled between ancient and modern thoroughfares, the river from a 'time / older than man', and the motor-hurled 'A' road. Here is a still point where time and eternity meet in a place forever giving birth to God's presence.

Though a place with 'no poems in it', the church of St Anno was, for Thomas, a counterpoint to the rest of life. Journeying briefly 'down the narrow path' on foot is a kind of defiance, with Thomas changing pace to turn, reach and enter the tiny church, and disengage from the hurrying of the outside world, the 'speeding / traffic I am part / of'. The simple and purposeful journey to this apparently unevocative place fills the first part of the poem with an understated clarity and crispness which somehow places the poet within the very practical movements of his time-bound journey, caught up in the speed of the road. In 'Llananno', though, a choice is hinted at which Thomas did not exercise at the beginning of 'The Bright Field' from the same collection. Now, instead of missing the moment, he 'turns down the narrow path', moving aside from the main trajectory of life, in a way he did not in the field; travelling then slowing and stopping, moving towards an experience of encounter.

The moment of stopping brings a change in the speed of the poem itself. The car is stopped. The poet walks. And the reflection from the river appears, as so often for Thomas, to be an image of inner reflection or seeking for God. And so we are drawn into a picture of Thomas entering a place that is apart from the bustle of life, and which may be a place of reflection – of seeing. And this movement is reinforced by the poet's use of language, shifting from bustling, crisp language in the opening lines ('often', 'no', 'gesture', 'speed') towards longer vowel sounds and soft consonants. 'I stop the car', he says,

> turn down the narrow path
> to the river, and enter
> the church with its clear reflection
> beside it.

Turn down; enter the church; clear reflection: gentler, more elongated, trailing sounds, demanding that we too slow down, as we receive this softer register and allow a change of pace to break over us. And then there is a break in the poem.

> There are few services
> now; the screen has nothing
> to hide.

Before the line break, Thomas is travelling and arriving; after the line break, he is present in this place of gentle epiphanies; but this is also a place of paradox. 'There are few services / now', Thomas says; few opportunities to encounter God through the kind of formal worship that takes place in the sanctuary of the church, so 'the screen has nothing / to hide'. This is the fifteenth-century rood screen, the jewel within this unremarkable, poem-less, largely Victorian church at Llananno. Carved figures of Christ and the apostles, mythical creatures and tumbling foliage, fruits and oak leaves, nestle in the screen in the modest church in the heart of Wales, speaking of centuries of worship and of an artistry that somehow defied the artistic destruction of the sixteenth century.[45]

But now, with so few services, the significance of the rood screen, which both concealed and revealed the sanctuary during the sacrament of the Eucharist, is lost. And if, with few services, there is now little to hide, then the screen is no longer a barrier between Thomas and the presence of God in the Eucharist. But there is a paradox here: the lack of church services diminishes the rood screen's purpose as a barrier between sanctuary and congregation, but it also means that the sacrament is less available and the need for a priest has diminished. And so Thomas (here more pilgrim than priest) is now brought 'Face to face / with no intermediary' between him and God. There may be no barrier in this little-used place of worship, but neither is there a bridge. Boundaries are blurred: 'access' to God is diminished and enhanced, and God is neither concealed nor actively brought before us.

And yet, there is a presence, because this is a marginal place, in which divisions and connections no longer have any meaning. The very presence of the screen speaks of the mystery and presence of God, so great, so potentially blinding and overwhelming, that we habitually shield ourselves from Him. And it is here that Thomas, stepping aside from the main journey into this marginal place, discovers God's presence in all His overwhelming gentleness.

Away from the speed of travel, Thomas encounters the mystery that needs time, space and contemplation to absorb. And while this moment is clearly fixed within time and the 'face to face' meeting between Thomas and God, this encounter with God suggests a timeless moment; the kind of timelessness that comes with intimacy, when the world falls away. Poetically, this is heightened by the river by the church and its 'quiet insistence on a time / older than man'. The ancientness of the river is a counterpoint to the timelessness of the moment; and that it is a reminder of 'a time / older than man', also stretches the sense of timelessness further, into a kind of prehistory, so that we are given hints both of time and eternity, dropping us more deeply into the timelessness of the moment.

This, then, is a journey stretching through time as well as along a road and beside a river, towards a timeless moment in

a timeless place, and towards the quiet epiphany of the poem's
final lines:

> ... I keep my eyes
> open and am not dazzled,
> so delicately does the light enter
> my soul from the serene presence
> that waits for me till I come next.

Finally, Thomas finds himself in a most intimate encounter with
God: but there is no burning bush, or clamour, or brightness
that accosts the senses. In 'Llananno', the presence is 'serene',
and simply fills Thomas's soul. And the final line suggests that
he knows that this is always available to him in Llananno,
where the 'serene presence' 'waits for [him]' until his next visit
to this place which has 'no poems in it / for [him]', but which
becomes a place of epiphany in a moment of stillness by the
ancient river, apart from the speeding road.

WEEK 4

Birthing

And she gave birth to her firstborn son and wrapped him in bands of cloth, and laid him in a manger, because there was no place for them in the inn. (Luke 2.7)

Week 4 – Birthing

Day 1

The Un-born

I have seen the child in the womb,
neither asking to be born
or not to be born, biding its time
without the knowledge of time,
model for the sculptor who would depict
the tranquillity that inheres
before thought, or the purity of thought
without language. Its smile forgave
the anachronism of the nomenclature
that would keep it foetal. Its hands
opened delicately as flowers
in innocency's garden, ignorant
of the hands growing to gather them
for innocency's grave.
Was its part written? I have seen
it waiting breathlessly in the wings
to come forth on to a stage
of soil or concrete, where wings
are a memory only or an aspiration.

The Un-born

A scan, and the first fluttering pulse of a baby's life gradually emerges through grainy black and white striations, into shapes and shadows, movements and curves which foretell the child to come. As yet unconscious of all around, but receiving sustenance pouring through a life-giving mother, this new life reaches into unformed, forming bone and flesh, and gradually takes shape.

Or a song – the psalmist's song, crooned like a reverse-lullaby:

> For it was you who formed my inward parts;
>   you knit me together in my mother's womb.
> I praise you, for I am fearfully and
>   wonderfully made.
> Wonderful are your works;
> that I know very well.
> My frame was not hidden from you,
> when I was being made in secret,
>   intricately woven in the depths of the earth.
> (Psalm 139.13–14)

Scan and psalm can both invite us into the fragility and strength of new life, caught between conception and birth; life travelling in tender darkness towards the raw brightness of earthly life.

As we begin this week of birthing, Thomas's 'The Un-born' also captures new life, suspended between conception and birth. It captures a moment both in time and out of time, caught between purity and fall, innocence and wounding, and it brings us a picture of life on the edge of consciousness, creativity and destruction.

As so often in Thomas's poetry, the title itself hints at the rich mix of meaning and association that he brings to a poem. This is 'The Un-born', with an all-important hyphen. 'Unborn' might suggest that we are in the company of a being '*not yet* born', but '*Un*-born' brings a broader, richer and more scattered patchwork of meanings. *Un*-born could be a stronger version of 'not *yet* born', or more emphatically, a being who is '*not* born' at all. Even more emphatically, this could be a picture of complete stillness; almost pre-creation, pre-thought, pre-language; or, in the tradition of 'un-saying', it could even suggest something that could reverse the birth process. This '*Un*-born' creature seems to hover on the very brink of life, in a way that can only be described as 'not' what it might be. It seems to occupy a liminal place.

And yet, as the title also emphasizes the word 'born', and as the whole poem circles around life in all its incipient beauty, it seems that Thomas is pointing to opposite meanings even in the one word, both saying and unsaying something at the same time. He speaks words that bring something into new life, while also saying the opposite, so new meaning is brought shimmering into life in few words. There is delicacy here, and there is strength in this soon-to-be product of the artist (or of God), who is both bearer and midwife of the new life, poised between the creative impulse and the creative act:

> model for the sculptor who would depict
> the tranquility that inheres
> before thought, or the purity of thought
> without language.

And then Thomas moves us gently towards the potential of this life, and its slow humanity, first with a smile, in the curious words:

> ... Its smile forgave
> the anachronism of the nomenclature
> that would keep it foetal.

The anachronistic 'nomenclature' which would 'keep it foetal' is one of Thomas's curiously circuitous phrases, which might cause us to falter – and which we might linger over a while to absorb. Perhaps it is the title of the poem which seems to be anachronistic; the emphatically named 'Un-born' no longer makes sense, and holds in a foetal state this new life which takes shape and moves towards birth. There is, after all, a strange new consciousness here, in the recognizably human 'smile' and an impulse to 'forgive'. And slowly, in language pregnant with paradise and its loss in the vagaries of life, this new infant's

> ... hands
> opened delicately as flowers

in innocency's garden, ignorant
of the hands growing to gather them
for innocency's grave.

In the tragedy of any new life, there is an innocent lack of understanding that this innocence will be lost and the paradise of womb-safety, of infancy, will be abandoned; there is no consciousness in the new life, of future loss. Hands that open towards life will be taken by 'hands growing to gather them / for innocency's grave'. And a question that Thomas asks might be one that we all ask about our life: 'Was its part written?' Is this creature, hovering between conception and lived life, about to embark on a path that is already shaped and contoured by the creator and sustainer of life, and will this in turn be shaped by the ground on which we find ourselves walking and the life we lead?

> ... I have seen
> it waiting breathlessly in the wings
> to come forth on to a stage
> of soil or concrete, where wings
> are a memory only or an aspiration.

Breathlessly because the new life does not yet need to breathe, or because this life waits in rudimentary, semi-conscious trepidation, or as one might wait to play life's starring role, the infant will land on 'soil or concrete', as if in a contemporary reworking of the parable of the sower. To emerge on to soil would seem to augur a life of growth, grounding, fertility; but concrete might equally lie ahead. And perhaps it is in any human life, or perhaps more particularly in a life lived on concrete, that we might lose memory, sight or consciousness that we are God's creatures – until we return to Him.

To linger over 'The Un-born', and allow it to interrogate us, may be to reflect on the life to which we have been called, and into which we have been born. As for the new life in 'The Un-born', our human life is an earthed life, placed in time and surrounded in the holy.

We might wonder how the writing of our part in life's drama weaves with the ground in which we have tried to put our roots, whether soil or concrete. And we might ask ourselves again, especially at this time of God's birth and new life in Christ, whether the ground in which we are rooted is the most fertile and productive ground in which we can live out a life wrapped up in God. We might see, in 'The Un-born', Christ waiting to enter our lives; God completely surrendered to the fragility of human life, caught in a moment of un-knowing, slow stretching, as uncertain and certain as all of us of the part we are to play. Utterly present to what is, and utterly limited to the unconscious flutterings of new unformed life.

In this week of birthing, this child, caught in a moment between beginnings and endings, 'biding its time / without the knowledge of time', preparing for soil or concrete, may be any of us. This child, where 'wings / are a memory only or an aspiration', may be the Christ, who has come among us and who will be born again.

Week 4 – Birthing

Day 2

Blind Noel

Christmas; the themes are exhausted.
Yet there is always room
on the heart for another
snowflake to reveal a pattern.

Love knocks with such frosted fingers.
I look out. In the shadow
of so vast a God I shiver, unable
to detect the child for the whiteness.

Blind Noel

Peppered through Thomas's poetry, are brief, pithy, chilly verses
of Christ's birth.[46] Filled with the bite of a Welsh Christmas,
the austerity of bleak frosted hills and hardy weather-beaten
worshippers trudging towards bread, wine and pain, these
poems of snow, light and darkness overlay the season of joy
with the agony of living. If there is a manger, it is empty; if
stars, they light the metallic hardness of the land. If there is
red, it is the colour of blood as much as robins or holly berries.

This can seem less than joyful. And yet these are poems of
Christ's birth. And what they offer, in strange and topsy-turvy
ways, is a vision of Christ born in ordinary scarred lives, and
to chilled hearts struggling to receive offered love, or uncon-
sciously accepting offered crumbs. 'Blind Noel' is one of these
poems – and in its chilly verses we find the camera turned on
Thomas himself, in a poem that is at once challenging, disturb-

ing and hopeful, and which takes us far beyond any clichéd or sentimental rendering of the Christmas scene.

The title of the poem is enough to warn us that this is Christmas, but not as we usually think of it. 'Blind Noel' is an example of how Thomas uses language, placing together words that do not really seem to fit, and in so doing causes us to stop and linger; to struggle, perhaps, and scratch our heads about its meaning. This language might cause us to worry, from the outset, that our expectations are not about to be fulfilled; how can 'noel' be blind, and what does it mean? This is language that cannot easily be translated into other words; it is paradoxical, 'unstable and dynamic',[47] language, to borrow a phrase from Michael Sells, which brings us up short. And all of this prepares us – invites us – into some kind of conversation with what is to come, as our minds, taken off track from commonplace or easily understood associations, slow down and open up to something new; if we surrender our *need* to understand, that is. And here, in this surrender, we might find that wonder lies: 'not in what the words mean, but in our being moved by what we cannot explain in other terms'.[48]

To move beyond the title of the poem is to discover a mix of wonder, weariness, love, creativity and frozenness, and an immanent, transcendent God. The themes of Christmas, we immediately hear, 'are exhausted'. The joyful, fearful thrill of the shepherds is worn out; the soaring angelic hosts bringing good tidings of great joy are too familiar, and richly evocative gifts of gold, frankincense and myrrh, have come to be a cosy exchange of Christmas gifts. All have lost their ability to thrill, Thomas seems to say, to bring God before us in wonder, love and praise. And yet, beyond the familiar, 'exhausted' themes, there is the hint that there is something more vivid, varied and piebald to be revealed. There is, says Thomas,

> ... always room
> on the heart for another
> snowflake to reveal a pattern.

These are curious lines. Even to mention snow, such a familiar staple of a Christmassy atmosphere, is to use one of the old, 'exhausted' themes. And snowflakes too can seem like domesticated and cosy pictures of the bleak midwinter. But somehow Thomas also seems to reach into and beyond the traditional snowiness of Christmas, and what this conjures up for us. Beyond what is easily understood, we are shown that it is the heart that apprehends. The heart can be open to receive new and unique revelations; new pictures of God, perhaps; new understandings of what it means to receive God-with-us in Christ. Exhausted though Christmas themes are, sentimental and hackneyed though they can be, the human heart has the ability to surrender to unique manifestations of God's presence, and respond uniquely, just as each unique snowflake reveals a pattern.

And then Thomas pushes us – pushes our hearts – to receive just such a new picture of God at Christmas; an immense God with the power to touch and to challenge:

> Love knocks with such frosted fingers.
> I look out. In the shadow
> of so vast a God I shiver, unable
> to detect the child for the whiteness.

God reaches out and challenges us with the immensity of a love that cannot be tamed. Not the loving, summoning touch of warmth and comfort which fits in with a vision of a personal God, but the overwhelming sudden charge of 'frosted fingers', of a ferocious love, which knocks on the door of our hearts – or buffets us with cold. And what is the 'such'? An emphasis, perhaps, of 'frosted' ('Love knocks with *such* frosted fingers'), or a reference to the snowflakes of the earlier verse: God may touch us with the unique patterning of the snowflake, and reach *us* in our uniqueness. However we read this phrase – however these words *reach* us – this God is an overwhelming, awe-inspiring midwinter God, whose immense, ferocious love somehow has a neutrality that goes beyond the personal and 'claimable'. God simply 'is', and the call may be not to domesticate this God but to recognize both the vastness that takes us beyond the individual, and the immense blinding whiteness that is difficult to look at; which makes us 'shiver' as it stretches ahead of us. This may be the brightness and ferocity of God's grace which overshadows us and calls out a response of awe; a frisson of fear, as we discover its ferocious life. Dare we look into so blinding a whiteness, and recognize God's enormity as well as God's presence in the life of an infant? Can we discover uniqueness in the midst of God's vastness – in each snowflake that constitutes the whole?

'Love knocks with such frosted fingers.' One invitation in this time of new birth is the invitation to bring to birth a new vision of God and a new understanding of grace, which reaches beyond our familiar expectations of God at Christmas, and the unconscious pictures we carry of God's love. 'Blind Nocl', which floats for us the possibility of a richer, more immense and less easy vision of God's presence at the incarnation, might lead us to ask questions about what happens when love comes knocking for us; when the Christ child leads us into the enormity, ubiquity and brilliance of God's presence.

Week 4 – Birthing

Day 3

Nativity

Christmas Eve! Five
hundred poets waited, pen
poised above paper,
for the poem to arrive,
bells ringing. It was because
the chimney was too small,
because they had ceased
to believe, the poem passed them
by on its way out
into oblivion, leaving
the doorstep bare
of all but the sky-rhyming
child to whom later
on they would teach prose.

Nativity

To enter the world of the nativity in Thomas's poems is to enter a world far away from cherished learnt stories of crib-cosiness. Adoring warm-breathed animals, haloed parents, the peace of a newborn infant are seldom to be found, and soft swaddling, soft breath, soft sighing or lullabying are rare.

Of course, Thomas's nativities depend for their impact on a shared heritage of Gospel narrative, centuries of tradition and the Christmas of memory, which have so shaped our imaginations. It is *because* of this rich tradition that a Thomas nativity can be so shocking when we first meet it. It is because we expect the glow of the stable, awestruck shepherds, the watchful adoration of Mary and Joseph and the peaceful slumbering infant, that a Thomas nativity, sometimes with a changeling in the manger, a machine all cogs and hard edges, can be so startling. It is *because* we expect starlight that the dropping of acid rain through a hole in the stable roof is so abrasive, and that when the gentle light of a halo is replaced with an irradiated glow, we are blinded and scalded by the vision. It is as if for Thomas all these shocking aberrations of the holiest of nights point out to us how we have replaced Christ with idols and objects of our own veneration.[49] What we have come to cherish – to idolize – is the fruit of our own ability, says Thomas, and this is at once creative, and also terrifyingly destructive. And yet we are shocked when we peep into the stable, and peer into the manger expecting to find the Christ child, only to be confronted by deities of our own making, in which we have come to place our faith. And so to reflect on Thomas's nativity poems, some of his poems of 'birthing', can be demanding and challenging. It can require of us courage and honesty as we see reflected back to us our own venerated gods.

But not all Thomas's nativity poems speak of a changeling machine, and today's poem 'Nativity', takes us into different territory. Rather than a mirror to our own destructive abilities, 'Nativity' has a simple majesty about it, a poignancy and even a gentle humour. It is Christmas Eve, we are told, with an unusual exclamation mark, striking an untypical note of breathless excitement. This is a time of waiting for magic to happen, and in the clangour of ringing bells, poets wait for the muse to strike, ready again to tell the great story of the incarnation; ready with 'pen / poised above paper' to write the Word in words – to capture the poem as it is born. Is this only the poem that the five hundred aspirational poets hope to write, or is the poem Christ Himself? For Thomas, Christ could be seen as a poet,[50] but also as 'God's metaphor'.[51] For Thomas, to call Christ 'God's metaphor' is not to suggest that He is 'just' a picture of God, a simile rather than God Himself. It is to find a way of expressing that Christ was and is the living expression and embodiment of the whole of God; a fully rounded, rich and utterly complete expression of all that God is, just as the best poetic metaphor tries to express that which cannot be expressed in any other way than in the word itself. So Christ is the Word who cannot be captured or turned into easy expression.[52]

The beginning of the poem is all speed and anticipation, heightened by the gentle plosive sounds of 'poets', 'pen', 'poised', 'paper' and 'poem', pushing the air out and forward in mini-explosions of breath and sound. But no sooner have the bells rung than the mood changes. In only the second sentence of the poem, the anticipation and forward movement is over, and so sudden is the change that we barely even notice that the moment has passed in a heartbeat, and we have already moved on to the reasons why the moment has passed, and the poem has slipped by unnoticed. Or are they excuses?

> ... It was because
> the chimney was too small,
> because they had ceased
> to believe, the poem passed them
> by ...

The 'chimney was too small', we are told: the traditional route for Christmas magic, guiding the spirit of Christmas into the heart of the house, is not substantial enough to accommodate the vastness of the poem. The poem, with all the overtones of the incarnate Word, cannot be channelled in ways that tradition demands and that we expect, and so it simply moves on, to other routes, other places into which to pour itself. And we are left to picture five hundred poets, still peering, still expectant, but looking in the wrong direction and unable to catch the poem on its way, with all the gentle poignant humour of this image in our minds. But then perhaps, suggests Thomas, the poem passes them by because of simple lack of belief, a paradoxical human failure to accept and receive the very thing for which we yearn. No wonder the poem escapes and goes its way, uncontainable, unfixable in words, and unnoticed by unbelieving poets.

But if the poets have failed to see the rich beauty of the poem, which 'passe[s] them / by on its way out / into oblivion', it seems that the incarnate God is persistent enough to arrive on the doorstep, which, we are told in a curious, shimmering and resonant phrase, is bare of all 'but the sky-rhyming / child'. There is a magical quality about this description, and the temptation may be to try to explain it and pin down the meaning, like a landed butterfly, but this may be to miss its point. These are words to ponder, beautiful in their simplicity, rich and complex in their allusive power, and if we linger over them we might each discover different meanings, different associations and emotions attached to them. Perhaps we might find an intimacy in this child left on a doorstep; a vastness in 'sky-rhyming;' a lilt in this internal rhyme which amplifies depth and breadth; which holds together the transcendent and immanent; the poem and child. Whatever the resonances to be found in these words, how fitting that in a poem of poetry and of the incarnate Word, there is a phrase for the incarnate one which defies easy understanding, but is loaded with rich and evocative meaning. A metaphor of God.

And yet, poignantly, even those tasked with the responsibility of speaking the poetics of faith, of giving poetic life to the incarnate one, will, in their impoverished understanding, succumb to the impulse to 'teach prose' to this meaning-defying poem-child. It is the language of clarity rather than an acceptance of the unsayable which wins out, even with the poets.

And what about us, as we draw near to the birth of the incarnate God, and open our lives afresh to His birth within us? Have we reduced the poem to prose? Are we tempted to name and pin down the incarnate one so that we can grasp and understand rather than allow the Christ child to live and breathe within us? Is our temptation to shape the newborn to fit our lives, our world, rather than allow the infant to shape us? Are we able to learn poetry rather than teach prose?

Are we able to allow the sky-rhyming child to baffle us, fill our worlds, draw close to us, breathe new life and faith into us?

Week 4 – Birthing

Day 4

Top left an angel

Top left an angel
hovering. Top right the attendance
of a star. From both
bottom corners devils
look up, relishing
in prospect a divine
meal. How old at the centre
the child's face gazing
into love's too human
face, like one prepared
for it to have its way
and continue smiling?

Top left an angel

Reading 'Top left an angel' is a little like staring at an old master: a medieval nativity scene, wrought in words, beautifully framed and filled with tokens of Christ's birth, including the unnamed mother and child. It is a reminder that Thomas's poetry is filled with echoes of the visual arts, that he explored artistry in all its forms, and associated God and Christ with artistry. 'God is an artist', he said; 'Christ was a poet.'[53] What God most 'conforms to', he says in his second poem called 'Emerging' (tomorrow's poem), is art, and in a number of his poems he reflected on great works of art. Works by Gauguin, Monet, Manet, Degas, Cezanne, Van Gogh and others, all fell under the idiosyncratic scrutiny of a poet who saw intimations of death in Jongkind's 'Beach at St Adresse', and who gazed at the gazers in Manet's 'The Balcony'.[54] Great paintings were reflected upon, walked around, and became the subject of Thomas's, and our, gaze, with his own imaginative vision turned into verbal attentiveness, rich with his own direct response and inviting us into an encounter with a moment of stillness in paint.

But 'Top left an angel' is entirely different. This poem does not describe a specific image, but it invites us into a verbal picture that calls to mind paintings we might have seen and books we might have read. The figures are never named and the moment described is never stated, but the signs and symbols describe and conflate moments of the nativity, and draw associations that turn this brief poem into a rich jewel, gathering and scattering light. More than this, the poem reaches beyond the nativity and into the Passion; beyond the birth of Christ and into the nature of human and divine love.

An angel appears in a corner at the top of the scene, as in any number of medieval and renaissance nativity scenes; a harbinger of good news to the shepherds, hovering in a moment of stillness and movement. And a star, looking forward to the coming of the Magi, signals that we have been called to the place of Christ's birth; and so early on in this scene, in just a few deft strokes, we are shown a collapsing of association from different elements of the birth narratives – symbols of holiness, good news, and of the call to journey to this place. But the tone darkens quickly, and within a few lines angelic light at the top of the scene is shadowed by devils looking upwards, 'relishing / in prospect a divine / meal'. Suddenly we are in the territory of Botticelli's *Mystic Nativity*, with its depiction of angels and devils, both celebration and judgement. And there are also hints of foreboding, as the infant Christ lies on a shroud, as if to point forward to the end of His earthly life.

But if in Botticelli's *Mystic Nativity* the demons already seem to have been defeated, as they are led away by angels and disappear back into the underworld, in Thomas's poetic depiction, the drama is still to be played out. And what might happen seems to be up for grabs – to the devils at least. They are hopeful, 'relishing' what might lie ahead for them. So it is not any demonic retreat or defeat that tells us how the drama will unfold. Instead, the image that begins in the middle of the poem, aptly with the word 'centre', points us to what will come to pass:

> ... How old at the centre
> the child's face gazing
> into love's too human
> face ...

Here, Thomas deftly draws us to one spot. 'Top left', 'top right' and 'bottom corners' have served to draw our attention to this central drama – to the divine event. But we are not called to the central image straight away; we are first captured and led by a curiously questioning adjective ('How old') even before we encounter the child's face, which is subject and object in this human–divine gaze; the new, ancient face of Christ. And then we find ourselves in the very heart of the poem. This is the look between infant and mother, in which we find depicted the story of human redemption. There are echoes here of another depiction of the nativity in art. In Piero de la Francesca's painting *The Nativity*, the heart of the depiction is again the relationship between mother and child. In the painting, Mary gazes upon Christ and prays before Him: but it is unclear whether she is praying *for* her infant, as any new mother might, or *to* Him, in adoration and heartfelt understanding of the enormity of this new birth.

In 'Top left an angel', however, it is the child who is gazing at the face of His mother; but that this is a newborn, as yet unfocused, plays again with time and eternity. 'How old' we are asked, is this child who can already gaze into the loving face of its mother? And then we learn that it is not only sight but *insight* that marks out this newborn, eternal child, who gazes into 'love's too human / face'. The face of His mother, we hear, is not just human, but *too* human. This is a love that is full, flawed and vulnerable. Or we might think of a love that is needy or limited; conditional or selfish, unable perhaps to see beyond the immediate; willing to embrace openly a new life, but discovering the cost of this in a way that is shocking, challenging and profoundly painful. We may see in this our own capacity to love, in all its limitations and glorious generosity, and we may see the love of a mother with presentiments of what is to come.

This human love is Mary's, but so too is it ours: all of our human loves and loving, all our hurts, needs and pains. And so too may this be human love through all of time, with its yearnings, desperation to *be* loved, and inability fully to grasp the grace, beauty and fearfulness of divine love. And the child who looks – who gazes – into 'love's too human / face', sees all this, and sees beyond it all. The gazing child, it seems, is already 'prepared' for the vulnerabilities and frailties of human love to 'have its way', and is prepared to 'continue smiling', even in the face of destruction. The wisdom of the Christ child brings awareness that the love into which He has cast Himself is a perilous place, but that divine love will continue, even as His earthly life is destroyed in the folly, confusions and destructiveness of others. But as with all Thomas's poetry, there are ambiguities that invite us into different ways of reading what is before us: read this poem again, and we might find, in the ambiguity of Thomas's language, that it is the child's *mother* who is prepared, in her 'too human' love, for the child whose life she has borne to have its way.

This brief, powerful poem-painting reminds us of the subtlety of Thomas's vision of the nativity; to mark Christ's birth is, for Thomas, also to be reminded of its purpose. We are not allowed to linger in the sentimentality of the manger, or even be shown the glories of the incarnation without being pointed to the Passion ahead. Glory and shadow go hand in hand, and yet the perilous-seeming ambiguity at the beginning of this poem, when it seemed it was all to play for as far as the devils were concerned, does not remain intact by the end. The darkness may relish 'a divine / meal', but even the deepest of shadows will not prevent the final smile of divine love.

There is ultimately something profoundly hopeful in this poem, which takes away none of the foreboding of what lies ahead. We are shown that in all the pains, glories and bright shadows of life, divine love will remain, and 'continue smiling'. Not because being born to Christ's life comes without consequences, but because in the story of God's self-giving, Christ surrendered Himself to the totality of human life, so that even its deepest shades and shadows are caught up in the life of God in Christ. One invitation to us, then, during this season, is to be born to the full meaning of Christ's birth. And in so doing, to accept the totality of our own lives, with all their pains and glories. And to know that at the heart of all is the eternal face of God: gazing upon us, with unending love.

Week 4 – Birthing

Day 5

Emerging

Well, I said, better to wait
for him on some peninsula
of the spirit. Surely for one
with patience he will happen by
once in a while. It was the heart
spoke. The mind, sceptical as always
of the anthropomorphisms
of the fancy, knew he must be put together
like a poem or a composition
in music, that what he conforms to
is art. A promontory is a bare
place; no God leans down
out of the air to take the hand
extended to him. The generations have
watched there
in vain. We are beginning to see
now it is matter is the scaffolding
of spirit; that the poem emerges
from morphemes and phonemes; that
as form in sculpture is the prisoner
of the hard rock, so in everyday life
it is the plain facts and natural happenings
that conceal God and reveal him to us
little by little under the mind's tooling.

Emerging[55]

> Every block of stone has a statue inside it, and it is the sculptor's task to discover it.[56]

Where and how do we expect to encounter God? We might think of prayer as the natural place of encounter. Or we may choose to enter a 'thin place' or space; we may expect to meet God in the unfamiliar or in ancient revelations. Our God might be transcendent or immanent; far from us, or close by; beyond all things, or profoundly present; quickening all things, far and near. We may not think of 'encountering' God at all, but more of revelation. Or we may even think of birth; of God being born in us and to us.

Thomas's second poem 'Emerging' is a poem of God discovered, and endlessly born to us, as much as encountered: born in the matter of the world and in the stuff of life; in rock and word, thought and art; in nature, in ordinariness, in our distillation and reflection on all that makes for daily living. It is rich with artistic association and heart-stopping phrases which might challenge us, draw us on, guide us through to a new vision. And so to read 'Emerging' (1978) is to allow something to emerge.

The poem opens in a very Thomas-like way, hinting (in the words 'Well, I said') that he is already in the middle of a thought or conversation. Fittingly for a poem called 'Emerging', even this opening leans towards a vision of God being brought forth from the depths rather than being met on edges, or momentarily touched from afar: God has not, despite Thomas's musings, 'happened by' on 'some peninsula / of the spirit,' a peninsula which may suggest the lean finger of the Lleyn, or any spare, fleshless place, somewhere separate from the rest of life. But as well as spare and lean, Thomas seems to suggest, we can also find a place like this comforting and familiar. And so 'It was the heart / spoke', out of some deep emotional commitment to the idea that God must be somewhere 'out there' – far from us, on 'some peninsula / of the spirit'. But, Thomas goes on, 'A promontory is a bare / place', and in a picture that conjures up a divine–human touching, reminiscent of Michelangelo's *The Creation of Adam*, he adds that

> ... no God leans down
> out of the air to take the hand
> extended to him. The generations have
> watched there
> in vain.

It is 'fancy', he says, which leads us to make God man-shaped, leaning down 'out of the air'. We are called to a different vision, of a God who is laid before us as the poem unfolds, in the same way that Thomas suggests our God lays Himself before us and is born in all our comings and goings, our thoughts and feelings, events and experiences; the God who is, as Bishop John Robinson put it, 'the infinite and inexhaustible depth and ground of all our being'.[57] We are, says Thomas, in an extraordinary phrase, worthy of long-lingering, 'beginning to see / now it is matter is the scaffolding / of spirit'. There is a beauty of language and richness of association here. With a nod to the new physics, Thomas refers to the interdependence of body and spirit, and pulls us away from the still-haunting idea that our souls and bodies are only temporarily shackled together in life, and destined to split again at death. It is not spirit that magics matter into life, he says; rather it is matter that provides the building blocks, and the depths, in which the holy lives.

And so in 'Emerging' (1978) we are called not to strain towards some spiritual goal, or to stretch out to be touched by a man-shaped image of God. We are called instead to discover God in the creativity and quickening of life, revealed to us as by an artist who crafts and creates, and in so doing gives birth. Just as 'morphemes and phonemes', the finely textured building blocks of language, give birth to the larger sound, rhythm and shape of a poem, so God emerges through the minutiae of life. Just as a piece of sculpture, pre-existing in the 'hard rock' and in the mind of the sculptor, is released, shaped and revealed by the crafting of the artist, so God, embedded in the physical world, is released, shaped and brought to birth by the crafting, 'little by little under the mind's tooling'.

'Under the mind's tooling': these final words take us back to the beginning of the poem, when we heard that it is the mind that might redirect us away from old pictures of God 'out there' towards new pictures of an immanent God. There is a suggestion here of the importance of thinking; *intending* to create meaning and frame experience: but this is not the same as an intellectual mastering of God in the world. If anything, 'Emerging' (1978) suggests quite the opposite. The 'mind's tooling' might work on the 'plain facts and natural happenings' which 'conceal God and reveal him to us', like an artist's chisel shapes the 'hard rock', but it can no more determine or limit God than can a chisel determine the 'form in sculpture' which is struggling to emerge under the artist's hand.

The illusion of the mind's control, or complete understanding, must be turned upside-down, Thomas seems to say. We must be prepared to discover God revealed to us in 'everyday life', as we abandon old pictures and discover the God who is waiting to be born in word and stone; in blood and bone and earth and joy and grief. The God who is born in human life. The God who is born as an infant.

Week 4 – Birthing

Day 6

Other incarnations, of course

Other incarnations, of course,
consonant with the environment
he finds himself in,
animating the cells,
sharpening the antennae,
becoming as they are
that they, in the transparency
of their shadows, in the filament
of their calculations, may,
in their own way, learn to confront
the intellect with its issue.

And his coming testified
to not by one star
arrested temporarily
over a Judaic manger,
but by constellations innumerable
as dew upon surfaces
he has passed over time
and again, taking to himself
the first-born of the imagination
but without the age-old requirement of blood.

Other incarnations, of course

This week, we are moving towards the great celebration of Christmas: the celebration of God-with-us, born as an infant both fully human and fully divine – God incarnate, enfleshed. The very name of this celebration – Christ*mas* – points us towards its meaning and its impact. From the words at the end of the service (*missa* in Latin, or *Cristmaesse* in Old English), the word 'mass' marks the ending of worship and sending from the great celebration; sending us towards God and out into the world,[58] to share and to live in the light of this faith-defining, history-defining, world-defining story, which we tell again and again in myriad ways.

From incense rising like prayer, to the scent and light of the Christingle orange, from carols to worship songs, from the mysteries of eucharistic liturgy, to hands raised in supplication and prayer, the people of Christ are called together at Christmas to celebrate Christ among us and to be caught up in Christ's life. We are called to know ourselves as the community of Christ's people, shaped and transformed by His life, death and resurrection, and to live Christ's risen life in God's world. And that we do this year by year through word, ritual, song, scent, taste and picture, is a reminder that the incarnation that we celebrate in the particularity of God born as an infant, also seeps and strides throughout our world, in grace and gift, in flesh, fur, stone and steel; in the very materiality of our world. Ours is, Archbishop William Temple famously said, the most 'avowedly materialist' of all the great religions, with its 'own most central saying' that 'the Word was made flesh'. Ours is a faith that enshrines 'the reality of matter and its place in the divine scheme'.[59]

'Other incarnations' is one of Thomas's poems that reflects on this vision. Here, *the* incarnation and 'other incarnations' share a poetic stage, and weave together to describe a world saturated by the presence of God – in Christ – and flooding too through all creation. All things are the places of God's presence, and all things may express the glory of God incarnate. All of matter, Thomas suggests, is shot through with God who is 'consonant with the environment / he finds himself in'. There is no contradiction, no dissonance between God and context; the two are in harmony, of a piece with each other. And it is God who determines the 'thingness' of a thing, from the cells that God animates, to the 'sharpening' of 'antennae', so that they become the acute receptors that they are. These are, suggests Thomas, 'other incarnations', other enfleshments of God, who is the quickening essence and amplifier of even the most minute forms of life,

> that they, in the transparency
> of their shadows, in the filament
> of their calculations, may,
> in their own way, learn to confront
> the intellect with its issue.

The 'transparency / of their shadows' is a curious phrase. It sounds contradictory: a shadow that might more immediately bring to mind darkness, opacity, flatness and lifelessness is here transparent – clear, manifest, bright. So strangely, the 'transparency' of the shadow calls to mind a kind of bright presence in shadow form; a strange reflection of something that is cast in sunlight, like Henry Vaughan's 'dazzling darkness',[60] pointing to God's presence beyond our knowing, in all that is unseen as well as seen. And so Thomas appears to invite us deeply into the unseen areas of the world; into its substructures, in shadows and barely-there images cast by solid objects, in that which lies beyond our conscious minds; and in filaments – in threads, networks, conductors of an unseen presence, in the finely wrought spun thread of life, thought and presence. And then, in a baffling spin of words, we are offered a glimpse of these other incarnations meeting – confronting – the powerful, glorious and dangerous power of the human intellect. There seems to be a hint here that these other incarnations meet us with a reality that is beyond thought. More than this, there is a suggestion that, so deeply are these 'other incarnations' held within us, that the thoughts and heartbeat of God may meet and coalesce in our human intellect and understanding, and so confront, shape and inform our heart and mind. And so these other incarnations, the shadows and filaments that quicken us, might bring to surrendered minds and hearts the incarnate one, in lives shaped, crafted, inhabited and quickened by God, whose coming is 'testified to' not by the one star of the nativity,

but by constellations innumerable
as dew upon surfaces
he has passed over time
and again.

Then, in the final lines of the poem, we hear words that seem to *root* us in the mystery of the incarnation. In this God of the Passover who has 'passed over time / and again', and now takes 'to himself' not the first-born of the Egyptians, but the 'first-born of the imagination', we find echoes of the Word made flesh. Christ 'images ... forth'[61] the Father, as one writer puts it. Christ is and shows us God, at once fully human and a perfect expression of God's inner reality and heart, but 'without the age-old requirement of blood'. Here, along with the reference to Passover, 'Other incarnations' reminds us that this is the *one* incarnation that will bring to an end the ancient tyranny of blood sacrifice.

As we lean towards Christmas, this is a time to be alive to 'other incarnations' in our God-soaked world. But it is also the time to allow the heart-stopping reality of *the* incarnation to seep into heart and bones and blood, quickening our senses, filling our prayers and 'animating [our] cells'.

Week 4 – Birthing

Day 7

The Gap

God woke, but the nightmare
did not recede. Word by word
the tower of speech grew.
He looked at it from the air
he reclined on. One word more and
it would be on a level
with him; vocabulary
would have triumphed. He
measured the thin gap
with his mind. No, no, no,
wider than that! But the nearness
persisted. How to live with
the fact, that was the feat
now. How to take his rest
on the edge of a chasm a
word could bridge.
                He leaned
over and looked in the dictionary
they used. There was the blank still
by his name of the same
order as the territory
between them, the verbal hunger
for the thing in itself. And the darkness
that is a god's blood swelled
in him, and he let it
to make the sign in the space
on the page, that is in all languages
and none; that is the grammarian's

torment and the mystery
at the cell's core, and the equation
that will not come out, and is
the narrowness that we stare
over into the eternal
silence that is the repose of God.

The Gap

'The Gap', from Thomas's 1978 collection *Frequencies*,[62] might seem a curious choice for reflection during this week of looking at 'birthing'. With strong overtones of the Tower of Babel,[63] and an apparently grumpy deity resisting humanity's attempts to draw close, any relevance to the birth of Christ, or some spiritual birth of our own, might seem far distant. And yet the story that unfolds in 'The Gap' seems to reach into the story of God born among us; so too does 'The Gap' some-how communicate the mystery of God's birth in Christ. But to arrive at this mystery, we are asked to travel through a story of humanity's attempt to control, dominate and destroy the mystery of God, through trying to capture the word *for* God before the Word comes to birth and is made flesh.

'The Gap' opens with a start. God wakes to discover that 'the nightmare' is real: humanity has been encroaching on divine territory, gradually, gradually, 'word by word', naming all things and so, potentially, drawing level with God. So high has the Babel-esque 'tower of speech' grown, that just one more word remains before vocabulary has 'triumphed', before humanity has developed a language so sophisticated and final that God can be named and captured. And with this, humanity will have become equal to God; will have a God's control and a God's knowledge. And the last word waiting to be discov-ered and fixed by humankind, is the word for God; a definitive, final, controlling word of ultimate power.

This, we hear, would erode the space – the gap – between us and God, and God would be left trying to rest 'on the edge of a chasm a / word could bridge', suddenly vulnerable to control-hungry humanity. And when the gap closes, mystery flees and 'fact' has won, robbing the human heart of its yearning direction. The urgency of this threads through the contours and sounds of the first part of the poem. Words fly around in short lines; some are repeated, and often-staccato sounding phrases are hurled quickly in simple, sibilant, sharp words, sometimes with small plosive sounds, or a note of sharp fear: woke, word, fact, feat, rest, triumph, persist, gap, chasm, no, no, no.

But there is still time, God concludes, still time to stem the flow. And the pace of the poetry s-l-o-w-s. Lines relax, words lengthen, rhythms deepen and sounds soften, requiring space and time to be uttered. Because there is still 'by his name' in the dictionary a 'blank', even though we lurch voraciously towards God, driven by our 'verbal hunger / for the thing in itself'. And in this Kantian allusion, we hear the full throttle human desire to access and conquer God. We desire the *word*, but not just the word; we also desire the 'thing' to which the word alludes.[64] We want, says Thomas, to reach with language into that which is unknowable and mysterious. We yearn, understandably, to *know* God; to *name* God. But we also yearn to *have* God, and might even want to *be* God, by naming and claiming the 'thing in itself'.

For God, Thomas says, the solution is both to close the gap *and* to keep it open. And in lines rich with emotion, perfectly poised verbal timing, and swaying movement, we are told of God's strange and compelling action of birth and sacrifice:

> ... And the darkness
> that is a god's blood swelled
> in him, and he let it
> to make the sign in the space
> on the page

To linger over these words is to experience their power. The slow-to-express 'swelling' of blood at the end of one line is simply and quickly 'let' at the end of the next, filling the 'blank' in a central image of birth and sacrifice. Because here, in this central image of God letting God's own blood into the dictionary, we might find Christ: Christ come to us in blood, rather than ink; gifted to us – born to us – as Word rather than discovered by us as word. This is Christ offered to us in our hunger for God, in the blood of new birth and bleeding from the cross, eternally bridging the gap between God and humanity, but not allowing us to collapse this gap through easy knowledge. The Word is here made flesh, is born to us and dies for us, in a sign that far surpasses the power of human language, and swerves the traps we lay for it. The Word is more complex, less definable, more life-giving, less controllable than any word of our making, and the closing of a gap with a single word would, in the end, also be a fantasy of our making. Our search would have ended, but we would not have found the treasure we seek.

But God generously maintains the space, and the great paradox of the filled and empty 'blank' in the dictionary, which we try so hard to fill as knowledge-hungry, word-hungry, control-hungry humanity, is that it both keeps God's transcendent mystery and shows us the most intimate, immanent vision of God-with-us. Denied the possibility of pinning Him down and bridging the final gap with a word, we are drawn on in our search for God expressed in this profound, intimate, expressive 'sign' we have been gifted, wrought in blood, which is 'in all languages / and none; that is the grammarian's / torment'; unquantifiable and incomprehensible; unerringly present, but not definable by any dictionary. This is the sign that we cannot pin down or control, but which invites us to understand that the whole of life, from the furthest-flung star to the most intimate 'cell's core', is shot through with the presence of God.

Leading us from God's waking panic as humanity encroaches, 'The Gap' takes us through God's offering of life and blood, which both holds us close and keeps us distant enough to draw us onwards, in yearning search. Finally, we are left with 'repose' for the God whose invitation to us is infinite, whose presence is assured, and whose mystery, which is 'the narrowness that we stare / over into the eternal / silence', remains intact.

Ours is not to have the final word on God. Ours is to understand that God's birth and self-giving is the final Word.

WEEK 5

Seeing

'Master, now you are dismissing your servant in peace,
according to your word;
for my eyes have seen your salvation,
which you have prepared in the presence of all peoples,
a light for revelation to the Gentiles
and for glory to your people Israel.'
(Luke 2.29–32)

Week 5 – Seeing

Day 1

The Kingdom

It's a long way off but inside it
There are quite different things going on:
Festivals at which the poor man
Is king and the consumptive is
Healed; mirrors in which the blind look
At themselves and love looks at them
Back; and industry is for mending
The bent bones and the minds fractured
By life. It's a long way off, but to get
There takes no time and admission
Is free, if you will purge yourself
Of desire, and present yourself with
Your need only and the simple offering
Of your faith, green as a leaf.

The Kingdom

Some years ago, 'magic eye' pictures, or 'stereogram images', were all the rage. Books, posters, postcards of magic-eye images flew off the shelves. They became the subject of TV shows and countless articles and conversations, and small groups of people were to be seen standing in front of shop windows, staring lop-sidedly at the window display or gradually, slowly walking backwards, eyes fixed ahead. They were all waiting for the large colourful patterned pictures in front of them, flat, decorative but apparently meaningless, to resolve into coherent three-dimensional images.

And then there would be 'the moment', as giraffes, planets, dinosaurs, flowers, words, Big Ben, or anything else, would leap out of the flat image and present themselves, suddenly rounded, full and alive. Shrieks and smiles would erupt from those looking on when the image became clear; plaintive cries of 'why can't I see it?' or 'there it is ... no it's gone', when the image escaped the viewer. Those who saw an image leap out for the first time might stagger slightly (as I did) as the hidden image at the heart of the picture came to life, or topple with the shifting centre of gravity, as the rest of the world seemed momentarily to turn on its axis to accommodate a new reality. It was as if the 'real' world had lain dormant beneath a flat exterior, waiting to emerge if we allowed it to. Move too quickly and it would go again; try to fix it by simply staring, and it would either lose its power to disrupt and challenge, or, like a rainbow, disappear.

In the endless flow of articles and books written about the creation of magic-eye pictures, often explaining how to see them, all sorts of theories were put forward. Flat images would only become three-dimensional if our eyes were wired up in a particular way, was one view; we had to be predisposed to see things in this way. And then there were (and are) the theories that it is *how* we look, how we *see*, which determines whether the three-dimensional images appear or not. Suggestions ranged from the complicated choreography of looking at dots on the image, waiting until the number of dots changes from two to three, and walking away from the image, to the more simple instruction to look through the picture, towards a distant vanishing point.

Whatever the accuracy of these many theories, they seemed to have something in common: the idea that we need to change how we *habitually* hold an image in our sights: how we habitually *look* at something, and instead shift our perspective. Our gaze, rather than seeming to capture and dominate an image, must instead allow the image to emerge and to reach us. All of these require a letting go of the familiar. More dramatically put, they require a loss of control, so that our usual way of seeing the world is disrupted and our expectations changed.

And whether we can 'see' the three-dimensional image or not, the possibility is held out before us that surface can give way to depth, and our controlling gaze is not the last word in meaning. And if we accept this, we might be surprised as the world turns and something new is revealed.

This is the case in these days after Christmas. Now the call to see the world afresh, and to see it in all its depths, is heightened. We have been meeting with Christ in the incarnation, in the quickening of the tiniest and must vulnerable of forms, all at once poignant and explosive. We have been confronted by the reality of God with us, present to us, hidden and not hidden in our world; visible and beyond our vision, gazing back at us as we search our world with hungry eyes. In these days, with the Word freshly among us, we are called to allow our perspective to be disrupted, and to see, with the gaze of faith, into the depths of the incarnation. And Thomas, who is so often a poet associated with God's absence, offers us such a vision. For Thomas, it is God's ubiquity that confounds us: this every-where-God is *so* present, *so* embedded and *so* embodied, that we fail to see the divine textures that turn a flat, apparently random pattern, in the place of God's action. For Thomas, it is a shift of perspective, an acceptance of the disruptive and a move towards becoming receptive, which draws us close to God's presence. And a vision of God's kingdom, and his poetic landscape offers us, time and time again, rich glimpses of a world brought into startling life and focus through the incarnation.

'The Kingdom', perhaps one of Thomas's most direct and simple but also moving poems, offers just such a vision. As with 'the marriage of here and now' in 'The imperatives of the instincts', we find ourselves invited to a place that is here already, but in which everything we expect to see has been reversed, and loss, pain and poverty have been flipped upside down, as if the Lord of Misrule is holding court: 'the poor man / Is king', 'the consumptive is / Healed', and those who are unable to see are instead held in love's gaze. In *this* world, it is the broken and the hurt who profit, not the profiteers. This is a vision of the impossible and utterly possible, distant and close kingdom of God, which lies just beyond our grasp, but within our reach, in the depths of our world – and which was so deeply rooted in Thomas's understanding of God's kingdom. 'I firmly believe', he said in a 1972 interview, that 'eternity is not something over there, not something in the future; it is close to us, it is all around us and at any given moment one can pass into it.' This, he went on, is 'The Kingdom of Heaven', to which we are 'so close ... that we get these glimpses of it'.[65]

A glimpse. As so often with Thomas, how he writes his poetry draws out his meaning, and the sudden shift in perspective which jolts us into seeing something afresh, and which now reframes the far-distant as the here-now, pivots around the poem's volta. But this volta is not an obvious break, and no noisy announcement of a mood change. Instead, it gently calls us, in the middle of a line, to lay down one thought, breathe briefly, and pick up a new thought, which steers us towards the realization that this distant world is actually with us now:

> ... It's a long way off, but to get
> There takes no time and admission
> Is free.

It's a long way off, we hear, as in the opening line. And then we hear the crucial word: 'but'. This is the magic-eye moment, when the distant kingdom resolves into the here and now. And as with a magic-eye image, all it takes to step into this unreal, supra-real world is a willing surrender of control and expectation. But, unlike the magic-eye image, this surrender is the gaze of faith, and the reality that emerges is not the trick of the draughtsman. It is the gentle and thunderous presence of the God whom we so often miss, but who is present in fluttering flesh, in the churned mud of a farmyard and in the ocean's swell.

All it takes, says Thomas, to walk into this ancient, new world which is utterly familiar and utterly and radically grace-filled, is

> Your need only and the simple offering
> Of your faith, green as a leaf.

Week 5 – Seeing

Day 2

Tidal

The waves run up the shore
and fall back. I run
up the approaches of God
and fall back. The breakers return
reaching a little further,
gnawing away at the main land.
They have done this thousands
of years, exposing little by little
the rock under the soil's face.
I must imitate them only
in my return to the assault,
not in their violence. Dashing
my prayers at him will achieve
little other than the exposure
of the rock under his surface.
My returns must be made
on my knees. Let despair be known
as my ebb-tide; but let prayer
have its springs, too, brimming,
disarming him; discovering somewhere
among his fissures deposits of mercy
where trust may take root and grow.

Tidal

When I first visited the little church of St Hywyn in Aberdaron,
one of the two churches then in Thomas's final parish, the poem

'The Other' had pride of place near the entrance. My memory is of a large slab of slate, with near-Gothic writing carved into it, carefully crafted but also rough-hewn, as if hurled from the earth and scoured by the elements but shaped by a poet. Looking back it seemed perfectly to embody the mood of 'The Other': a brief, intensely powerful poetic evocation of the wild howling of a primal force, pounding in from the depths of the Atlantic and on to a spare outcrop of ancient rock, and our eternal crying out to God, figured in foaming waves, an unending rhythm of approach and falling away. 'The Other' is just one of Thomas's poetic hymns to the sea, that picture of eternity and power, with its endless roar and constant whisper, forever uncovering and reshaping the land.

It is little surprise that the ocean figured large for Thomas. The son of a mariner, going around ports as a boy and growing up on Anglesey, then later living close to the sea in Aberdaron, the sea's swell, sound and surge formed the backdrop to Thomas's life. Then in early retirement, hearing the breaking waves at Porth Neigwl ('Hell's Mouth') he was 'given the opportunity to return to his first love, the sea'.[66] Exulting in the flight of the sea birds chasing fish, he gloried in seeing 'a way of life which is indescribably older than us'.[67] And so in countless poems, the sea is a character populating Thomas's poetry. It is a primal place, a grave for islanders and a way of life.[68] It is a relentless backdrop, a picture of prayer, of the vast eternity of God, and of our yearning and perilous journey into God's mystery.[69] The sea, also ubiquitous eavesdropper on Thomas's life in his glorious prose/poetry collection *The Echoes Return Slow*,[70] rolls across Thomas's poetry, redolent of God, dangerous and life-giving, like the ocean itself, glittering and louring, yearning and bellowing; a magnetic, changeless force, which changes everything around it, and carries the heartbeat of faith.

'Tidal' is just one of Thomas's sea poems, and in it there is an echo of another great poem of faith and flow. Matthew Arnold's 'Dover Beach', that beautiful, painfully bleak vision, also tells of sea air, spray and the roaring sound of ancient rocks ground to shingle. In 'Dover Beach', crashing wave upon crashing wave, resolving into the retreating ebb tide, are a reminder of a previously full and now ebbing swell of faith, leaving a dark, joyless and loveless world. For Arnold, the sea-swell and beating of the waves take us on a poetic journey from calm and moonlight to struggle and turmoil. But, perhaps unusually for Thomas, the journey that he takes us on in 'Tidal' offers us something altogether more hopeful than Arnold's poem of the tidal ebb of faith: less a poem of the despair at retreating faith than a picture of surrender of the tides to the one who causes the waves to break.

The sea in 'Tidal' seems to take on another character again in Thomas's extended ocean metaphors. It is persistent and, like prayer and pray-er, it seems intent on discovering and revealing the depths of the shore, intent on laying bare what lies beneath and catching a glimpse of the foundations of the very earth 'exposing little by little / the rock under the soil's face'. The breakers' gradual encroachment on the land, echoing our own need to draw again and again towards God, offering all that we have and all that we are, suggests too our hunger to catch a glimpse of the God who has created and sustains us. Perhaps there are times when we pray that we find ourselves hoping that, by hurling our prayers with the vigour of breakers on a beach, the shingle, the messy surface of life, will simply be pulled away to reveal something pristine. Or will allow us to see God's face, free from the overlay of messy life.

But Thomas suggests that if we are to catch a true glimpse of God, it will not be through greedily grasping, or the 'violence' of our prayerful demands, because 'dashing / [our] prayers at him will achieve / little other than the exposure / of the rock under his surface'. Instead, it is through a kind of surrender that we might catch a true glimpse of God. 'My returns', says Thomas, 'must be made / on my knees'; it is through *offering* that we might know God, not through noisily demanding God's presence, and there is room for both the ebbing and brimming of prayer as we reach towards God. There may be despair in prayer, Thomas suggests, and we may feel that we are withdrawing from God (or God from us); our energy may drain away and be sapped, and we may struggle to find our way up the beach, or struggle to seek God's face.

But somewhere, too, we may discover that our prayer leaps and laps unbidden, probing, 'brimming' and 'disarming' God, and in the tidal flow of land on sea, of soil pulling back from rock, our vision of God may be subverted. Without forcing, we might glimpse not the bare rock face of an impassible God, granite-hard, smooth and unrelenting, but the cracked places of vulnerability, made fertile with 'deposits of mercy', which become for us a foundation for trust. It is in the cracks, Thomas suggests to us, that we catch a glimpse of our God who comes to us and meets us in the vulnerabilities of life. Just as Thomas sees and knows Jesus with His crucifixion wounds; and as Paul sees Christ even in his own blindness and even in his darkness of heart, we can suddenly catch a glimpse of the God who comes to us in gaps, crevices and cracks made rich with unsought grace. And we are called to resist the urge to pound God for a response; we are called to surrender and glimpse our God, caught in the tidal flow of our prayer, in the eternal and eternally vulnerable. In this season of God made known to us in the vulnerable Christ child, who will grow and suffer as we do, but who commands the waves and shapes the contours of our land in ways we can never know, we are called to discover the 'deposits of mercy / where trust may take root and grow'.

We can no more claim control of the land-hurled waves than we can command God. We have to wait. And rest. And discover the strength of God's mercy.

Week 5 – Seeing

Day 3

The Absence

It is this great absence
that is like a presence, that compels
me to address it without hope
of a reply. It is a room I enter

from which someone has just
gone, the vestibule for the arrival
of one who has not yet come.
I modernize the anachronism

of my language, but he is no more here
than before. Genes and molecules
have no more power to call
him up than the incense of the Hebrews

at their altars. My equations fail
as my words do. What resource have I
other than the emptiness without him of my whole
being, a vacuum he may not abhor.

The Absence

There is a story which Thomas often told. It is the story of
how, leaving the house one day to go visiting a farming family
who lived high in the hills, he saw a man in a field 'docking
mangels', hacking at a crop in the harsh agricultural uplands.
This was backbreaking work. But when he returned, later that
same night, Thomas saw the same man doing the same job in

the same field: bent, distant and intent only on this unforgiving task, in an unforgiving landscape.[71] And so the character Iago Prytherch was born, Thomas's ambivalent hero, anti-hero and poetic companion, a man of the hills, through whom the poet explored the doggedly enduring life of the Welsh farmers. More than this, it was through Prytherch that Thomas began in earnest to explore the ways of God to humanity in the inhospitable landscape of the bleak hills: who caused Thomas to ask questions about this God who seemed to demand so much of these noble survivors, these specks on the landscape, who seemed to live in so merciless a world.

So it was that a man docking mangels in a field contributed to Thomas's re-understanding of the world as a place of divine presence even in apparent absence – because exploring the ways of God to humankind meant, for Thomas, apprehending the world afresh. Often in his early poems, hill farmers, parishioners, even fellow clergy seem to exist in a state of isolation or suspension: surrounded by empty space, far distant in the hills, eking out a harsh life, or turning their face to the wall, inaccessible, or helpless in the face of apparent divine disinterest in the lonely lives of empty people. To read Thomas's poetry of empty space, such as 'Out of the Hills', 'A Priest to His People', 'A Labourer', 'Affinity' or 'Peasant Greeting',[72] is to discover a bleak and beautiful world, shot throught too with a plaintive, painful cry of isolation.

But slowly, slowly, reaching into the lives of his parishioners and exploring the God who gave them life, the empty spaces, the voids and gaps in Thomas's world gave way to places of presence. Discovering and describing the nobility of the hill farmer as in 'The Servant',[73] waiting on God in empty churches, as in 'In Church' or 'In a Country Church', and even plunging into his own interior world, as in 'This to do', seemed to shape Thomas: empty spaces became places of prayer and presence, humming with life. The hidden whisper, the blank sheet, the gaps between stars and the unaccommodated moment all remained spaces, but were no longer empty. And that God *maintained* space – kept a distance from humanity (as in 'The Gap'), even seemed to become for Thomas an act of love and grace: it is the gap, he suggested, which draws us on in love's slipstream, and in our yearning to follow the God we may only glimpse.

It took a re-visioning of God's world to discover presence in absence: to discover that apparent absence may be benign and loving presence. And 'The Absence', in which the imperceptible, indescribable and ungraspable God is revealed in invisibility, is one of Thomas's most well-known examples of how empty space can reveal as much as conceal God, and draw us into God's orbit, even though the key image is emptiness, extraordinary emptiness. 'It is this great absence / that is like a presence,' says Thomas in the opening lines, 'that compels / me to address it without hope / of a reply'. The great absence is God as distant, separate, intangible and leaving no clues, and the language used throughout the poem creates shapes around space where God is *not* to be found, moving us into a kind of void: there is a lack of hope, a failure of language to describe God, and the human experience of encountering nothing. But paradoxically, even in all this absence, we are left a powerful sense of God-with-us.

The absence, which is like 'a room I enter / from which someone has just / gone', is empty space with the imprint of a presence. And in typical Thomas fashion, the structure of the poem underlines its sense; there is a space – an absence – between the first two verses which emphasizes the space in the just-empty room. We are left in a liminal place, which may be a reception area, ante-room, waiting room, even an airlock between spaces, but it is emphatically where God is not; it is a

> ... vestibule for the arrival
> of one who has not yet come.

But the nature of the emptiness changes as the poem goes on. The first emptiness, the absence of verse one, 'compels' Thomas 'to address it', even though he is 'without hope'; he is drawn into the search for God by God's absence – through yearning, or need or desire, and arrives in the just-empty, about-to-be full 'vestibule'. It seems at first that Thomas is moving towards something, but there is nothing to arrive at.

By the third verse, there is a stationary quality to the poetry:

it is as if Thomas has stopped. I try to update my language, says Thomas, as if this could enable him to reach God, 'but he is no more here / than before'. Here is a profound surrender to the God beyond speech, as Thomas grapples with realizing that the God who is pursued, described and hoped for, does not bend to the pursuer. Even when drawn on by absence, Thomas knows he has no control over the finding of God: language, equations and rituals all fail if they are mere levers to pull in the quest for God. And a new kind of 'emptiness' emerges in the poem: Thomas's own emptiness, the 'emptiness without him of my whole / being, a vacuum he may not abhor'. With this distant carol-echo of the incarnation of Christ born to Mary, Thomas suggests that this emptiness is the only 'resource' he has, or that any of us has. This is a recognition that it is God who brings all and who responds to all. It is God who cannot help but live within and through us, as we grasp that we may be the 'vestibule' of God's presence.

By the end of this paradoxical, shifting poem, the movement towards the empty space, the vacuum, is reversed but not resolved. We are, with Thomas, drawn 'out' towards the beckoning emptiness of God's absence, before moving to the inner space which might, in our surrendered emptiness, draw the presence of God. But our experience of God pulls us both beyond ourselves and within; pulls us on to answer the beckoning call, and asks us to grasp that we are both searcher and 'vacuum he may not abhor'. In this extraordinary double pull, 'The Absence' paints a picture of God everywhere, at all times: or as Michael Sells puts it, a statement of transcendence (God's otherness) 'leads to an affirmation of radical immanence. That which is beyond is within. That which is other is the non-other.'[74] This is a vision of the world which may be grasped as we live in the light of the incarnation: a vision of God caught up in the exigencies, the glories, the frailty and the splendour of human life. And a vision of a world shaped and brought to life by the God who is so present, so compelling, that we follow only to discover that God has always arrived before us; never left us.

Tomorrow's poem, 'Adjustments', takes us deeper into this vision.

Week 5 – Seeing

Day 4

Adjustments

Never known as anything
but an absence, I dare not name him
as God. Yet the adjustments
are made. There is an unseen
power, whose sphere is the cell
and the electron. We never catch
him at work, but can only say,
coming suddenly upon an amendment,
that here he has been. To demolish
a mountain you move it stone by stone
like the Japanese. To make a new coat
of an old, you add to it gradually
thread by thread, so such change
as occurs is more difficult to detect.

Patiently with invisible structures
he builds, and as patiently
we must pray, surrendering the ordering
of the ingredients to a wisdom that
is beyond our own. We must change the mood
to the passive. Let the deaf men
be helped; in the silence that has come
upon them, let some influence
work so those closed porches be
opened once more. Let the bomb
swerve. Let the raised knife of the murderer
be somehow deflected. There are no
laws there other than the limits of

our understanding. Remembering rock
penetrated by the grass-blade, corrected
by water, we must ask rather
for the transformation of the will
to evil, for more loving
mutations, for the better ventilating
of the atmosphere of the closed mind.

Adjustments

A dripping tap which takes a day to fill a basin. A long journey which we travel step by step and suddenly discover we are arriving. A long-awaited event, which draws upon us second by second, minute by minute, even though we could never imagine it arriving. Grandmother's footsteps: a game of blink-and-you-miss-it movements, of turning and discovering, with thrill of excited fear, that the 'statues' behind have been approaching unseen. Adjustments. The merest adjustments to an apparent stillness, which tell us that something is happening.

We are familiar with the adjustments of everyday life, which, even when we are the movers – the agents – seem to emerge mysteriously, shockingly, as if from something hidden. Thomas's 'Adjustments' draws on this experience. But his adjustments are the actions of a hidden force not of our making: an 'unseen power'. Here, moments, miles, movements are all in the gift of the God whose cover of invisibility is blown not by grand gestures, not even by absence, but by activity that is so fine-grained as to be imperceptible. This is, for Thomas, the *deus absconditus*: the hidden God, a word rooted in *abscondere* (to hide away), who reaches back into the Scriptures, through Job who is unable to 'perceive' God, or 'behold him' (23.8–9), to Isaiah 'Truly, you are a God who hides himself' (45.15).

And in 'Adjustments', we are called to discover this 'hidden' God. In the first part of the poem, God is explored as a subtle, profound presence, weaving a barely perceptible path through the whole of life. This God who is not a being,[75] but caught in the realm of the barely visible, challenges our ability

to name Him, the one who for Thomas is 'never known as any-
thing / but an absence'. But this God is far from absent: living
in the 'adjustments' made deep in the warp and woof of the
world, as in the stone-moved mountains, or minutely threaded
garments, this God is hidden by the very subtlety and depth
of such profound presence, quickening all things; so embed-
ded and imperceptible that all can be experienced as an act of
grace. And so, paradoxically, God's presence is brought to our
vision by being profoundly hidden.

In the first part of the poem there is a busy-ness to the verse.
Before the break, which also brings a break in tone, the sounds
are sharper and slide over each other with sibilant ease, as if
we are moving, with the hidden God, through the depths of the
world. 'Absence', 'unseen', 'sphere', 'cell', 'catch', 'demolish',
'stone': the sounds tumble and elide. But then the tone begins
to shift as the poem's break approaches. The busy-ness eases,
the sounds soften and elongate ('gradually', 'thread', 'difficult')
as we move, or are moved, towards a new and deeper vision of
this God whom we 'can never catch / ... at work'.

The break itself signals a gentler soundscape to the poem:
gentle plosives, elongated sounds and the language of surren-
der transform the vision of God's adjustments, changing the
direction of the poem. We move from a sense of purpose and
movement in the first part of the poem to a profound sense
of surrender through which *we* are also affected by God's
adjustments.

> Patiently with invisible structures
> he builds, and as patiently
> we must pray.

'We must pray.' It is not for us to name God; it is not for us to
catch God at work, to see God busily moving rocks and draw-
ing threads. Instead, it is for us surrender to 'a wisdom that /
is beyond our own', and to pray. 'We must change the mood /
to the passive,' says Thomas, and from here the poet leads us
through a series of arresting images which may cause us to
stop, may challenge us and stretch us, and invite us to think

again about the adjustments wrought by God which shape our
world and which shape us, subtly and imperceptibly. 'Let the
deaf men / be helped', says Thomas, in an image that plays
with human and divine agency:

> ... in the silence that has come
> upon them, let some influence
> work so those closed porches be
> opened once more.

These adjustments, in which ears are unstopped through 'some
influence', may be the work of God, or the work of humanity:
the skill of the doctor may work with God's adjustments to
forge new possibilities for those 'closed porches', thresholds
to the world which have somehow become blocked. But these
'closed porches' may be more than purely physical. There is
also a hint of a kind of spiritual deafness: a reluctance to enter
the liminal spaces and become subject to God's gentle crafting
of matter, of heart and will. There is more than a hint here of
a challenge to us as we surrender to a 'wisdom that / is beyond
our own'. And the images that follow explore this further.

> ... Let the bomb
> swerve. Let the raised knife of the murderer
> be somehow deflected.

We are called to pray, says Thomas, but how often do we pray
for the adjustments that *we* want God to make. 'Make this
happen,' we may pray: stop the darkness, prevent the evil of
our world – 'adjust' things according to our will. But God is
not ours to order and God's adjustments are not at our control.
To pray for the bomb to swerve and the knife to be deflected
may seem to be prayers entirely in keeping with the flourishing
of God's kingdom – and yet. And yet there seems to be a sug-
gestion that our prayer for the bomb and the knife to miss their
mark may also be to miss the point about the deeper adjust-
ments which come with prayer. It is not for us, Thomas seems
to say, to determine God's adjustments to the flight of bomb or

knife, when it is the condition of the human heart which has already permitted that flight to begin.

The call is to adjust our vision of God: not just to spot where God has been, not just to discover God in the hiddenness of dextrous amendments, but to allow the 'loving mutations' that may take place within us. The call is to surrender to inner 'transformations of the will / to evil', which may be as demanding, as slow and as dextrously wrought as the shaping of rock by the gentle, imperceptible intensity of grass and water.

> ... Remembering rock
> penetrated by the grass-blade, corrected
> by water, we must ask rather
> for the transformation of the will
> to evil, for more loving
> mutations, for the better ventilating
> of the atmosphere of the closed mind.

This time of year, we discover the hidden God revealed to us in the form of a child, with all the rapid, subtle, profound adjustments that take place in the life of an infant. And we are reminded that this life came into being in the radical surrender of His mother, and will end in an even more profound and radical surrender of life to God. This is the heartbeat of the incarnation, and central to Thomas's vision: a vision of God-with-us in the cell and electron, and deep in the human heart. Thomas drew from the American writer Allen Tate to express the profundity and demands of realizing this vision: 'only persons of extraordinary courage and perhaps genius even', said Tate, 'can face the spiritual truth in its physical body'.[76]

This is a time for reflecting on the spiritual truth newly revealed in the physical body. This is a time for seeing our world afresh, in all its material glory, and knowing it as a God-filled place, shaped lovingly by minute adjustments.

Week 5 – Seeing

Day 5

The God

Of Poets

Made of rhyme and metre,
the ability to scan
disordered lines; an imposed
syntax; the word like a sword
turning both ways
to keep the gates of vocabulary.

Of Musicians

The first sound
in the silence; the frequency
of the struck chord; the electrical,
ultimate rhythm of the full
orchestra, himself the
conductor of it and the composer.

Of Artists

Who disguises
himself in wood and stone;
who has to be unmasked
with such patience; who escapes
in the end, leaving them standing,
tool in hand, in front of a supposition.

Of Scientists

The agitation at the centre
of non-being; the agreed myth
of their equations; the experiment
that proved them wrong; the
answer they have overrun
that waits for them to turn round.

Of Theologians

The word as an idea,
crumbled by their dry
minds in the long sentences
of their chapters, gathering dust
in their libraries; a sacrament that,
if not soon swallowed, sticks in the throat.

Who Is

Whose conversation
is the aside; whose mind
is its own fountain, who
overflows. Who takes the Cross
from between his teeth
to fly humanity upon it.

The God

We all see God in different ways. We discover the flickers, the glimmers, the lights and shades of God according to our lives, characters and contexts. And what most stirs our hearts and minds, what fires our vision and brings a sudden explosive picture of God before us, may show us something uniquely about how God works in the world – in *our* world. Is God revealed for us in the garden's bloom, or in the growth of a child, or in the alchemical transformations of ingredients into a memory-making meal? Perhaps we catch a glimpse of God in the intensely, exhaustively written code which brings film, ideas and news to life at the touch of a button, or in the words we write or speak, or in the music we hear, or the people we love.

'The God', from the 1992 collection *Mass for Hard Times* explores this theme. It shows us God living deeply in the form and structure of the poet's words and the musician's notes; in the revelation, through the sculptor's art, of sacred substance, and in the scientific revelation of life's energy. For Thomas, artistic creativity was always profoundly linked to God and divine creativity. In his introduction to *The Penguin Book of Religious Verse*, Thomas reflected on the poet as *intrinsically* religious. He echoed Coleridge in saying that 'the nearest we approach to God ... is as creative beings',[77] and that the poet *recreates* 'by echoing the primary imagination',[78] the creative force of God which brought all things into being, and which sustains and unifies all things. And we, as humans who are also capable of imagination and creativity, dimly echo in all our creative acts that great primary creativity of God. 'The world needs the unifying power of the imagination', said Thomas, and the 'two things which give it best are poetry and religion'.[79]

In 'The God', we are offered a vision of the God who lies at the heart of all life, of all actions and in all human crafting, but who also gives shape, order, containment to the explosion of creativity at the heart of the world. Micro and meta; uncontainable, untameable, revealed in what we shape, and shaping us as we do so. It is as if Thomas is taking the idea of the 'scaffolding of spirit' which appeared in 'Emerging' (1978) and stretching it, so that here God is not only the God of the sculptor's liberating art, or the poet's careful placing of sound upon sound, but is the God of the musician, and also the God of the scientist and theologian.

The themes that wind through the verses are both obvious and subtle. There is the theme of how God is bound up in our making, doing, crafting, shaping and thinking, and to read this poem is to discover *similarities* in how God is seen and known in all sorts of contexts. But there are subtle distinctions too, in our different ways of glimpsing God and *just* missing God's essence and depths. And there is also the theme of a God who *confounds* humanity in different ways at the very moment of revelation, because God can't, ultimately, be either captured or released by our glorious, but limited, grasp of the God who underpins all of our lives. The God of poets, musicians, sculptors, scientists and theologians is the same God; but in their – in our – different ways, we glimpse and miss God in all our endeavours.

As Thomas saw such a link between artistic endeavour and divine creativity, it is no surprise that in 'The God', the God of poets, musicians and artists is woven into the very fabric of what is being created, and so God shapes it too. In an image for the whole of our lives, this God creates, shapes and reveals all at once; is 'Made of rhyme and metre' or 'disguise[d] ... in wood and stone'; can 'scan / disordered lines' and is both 'conductor ... and composer' of the music, as well as its sound. The God of musicians is the 'frequency / of the struck chord', the background pulse and hum of life, so is depicted as working in, through and alongside us in all our creative endeavours. But the God of the artists cannot be *confined* by a poem or a piece of sculpture: this God eludes the sculptor as soon as the shape has emerged. God 'escapes / in the end'. Nor does God permit the language of the poet to open too easily into meaning: the poet's word is

> ... like a sword
> turning both ways
> to keep the gates of vocabulary.

God is the gatekeeper here, as if the word of God in the work of the poet conceals as much as it reveals. Whether this is deliberate, to prevent an easy expression of meaning, or because God can never be fully expressed, the God of the artists is unfixable and cannot ultimately be held or contained in any work of art.

But God is the God of scientists and theologians as well as poets, musicians and artists, and like the God of the artists, we hear, the God of the scientists inhabits the depths of the work. God is in the building blocks and in the invisible, apparently intangible formulae and is the pulse at the heart of the universe. In his 1978 collection *Frequencies*, Thomas wove an extended image of the immanent God, present in a network of equations and formulae, an intricate web of being on which all life depends, lying at the heart of the universe, expressed through numbers and figures rather than vocabulary, and he continued to explore this throughout his poetic life:[80] he did not just suggest that God is *in* science or *is* science, but that all things scientific, all the building blocks of life, and scientific endeavours are expressions of God at work. And so it is in 'The God', where the God of scientists *is* the 'agitation at the centre / of non-being', *is* the pulsing of life and somehow inhabits the very formulae that are embedded in the material world.

This God of the scientists is as visible and rooted in the creative and life-giving processes as the God of the artists and musicians; but there is a difference in how the scientists and artists catch a glimpse of God. If the God of the artists cannot ultimately be 'fixed', the God of the scientists tends to be *missed* – overlooked. God speaks in equations, experiments, and offers answers; but the scientists speed past them, eagerly rushing on, according to their own agenda. And so the God who offers them an answer, in the deepest equations, waits. God waits for the scientists to 'turn around' and see deeply and fully: waits for their *metanoia*.

In 'The God', though, it is the God of the theologians who is most likely to be 'missed'. Too much abstracted thought *about* God; too much intellectualization and too little lived reality *of* God, dries God out, and turns the living Word into an 'idea' only, 'crumbled' in the mind, and 'gathering dust'. This God becomes

... a sacrament that,
if not soon swallowed, sticks in the throat.

We run the risk, says Thomas, of simply losing sight of God if we become stuck in our theologies. God's glorious mysteries flee if our exploration of the living God becomes a quest for rigid meaning, limited by our own thoughts, literal and closely defined. We no longer catch a glimpse of the living God in the corner of our eye; we no longer feel the tug at the sleeve, or catch the scent of the Holy Spirit weaving through places and people. And all because we want to see too clearly, too starkly and too distinctly.

And then Thomas offers a final picture of God. This God is the source of all creativity and generativity, whose 'mind / is its own fountain'. This God is unconfined, subtle yet 'overflowing', and in its final image which is itself overflowing, 'The God' brings us redemption, new life in the cross, and the Word as a sword in God's mouth. This is the God

> ... Who takes the Cross
> from between his teeth
> to fly humanity upon it.

Allowing these final words to seep in can be a glorious surrender to the vibrant, dangerous, unfixable, risky, untameable, radical, grace-filled God, who beckons us, shows us our truth, waits for us in our rush, and resists our crushing rigidity. The God of the artist, the poet, the musician, the scientist and the theologian – the God of us all – is always offering us a glimpse of glory and leaving us hungry for more, is never limited to our vision, our understanding or our desires, and is never completed by our thoughts, our words, our actions.

Week 5 – Seeing

Day 6

That there ...

That there is the unfamiliar
too. That there is a landscape
that will through all time
resist our endeavours
at domestication. There is one
who models his disguises
without a thought, to whom
invisibility is as natural
as it is to be above
or below sound. He hides himself
in a seed so that exploding
silently he pervades the world.
He is the wilderness imprisoned
under our flagstones yet escaping
from them in a haemorrhage
of raw flowers. He bares his teeth
in the lightening, delivering
his electric bite, appals us
with his thunder only to unnerve us
further with the blessing of his held breath.

That there ...

There is something familiar about 'the unfamiliar' in this poem.
There are ideas about how God is revealed and made visible to
us; themes that we have encountered throughout these reflec-
tions, and especially during this week of 'seeing'. There is the

theme of a God who is hiding, which brings back to mind the *deus absconditus;* the 'hidden-away' God, who, like the word 'abscond', appears not just to be *hidden* but to have fled, as if avoiding our capture. And in a familiar Thomas way, the God in 'That there ...' is not only hidden, but is not named at all, and yet is unmistakenly brought before us. For all the familiarity of Thomas's way of offering us a glimpse of the unseen and an echo of the unheard God, this God seems to be different. From its first line, to some of its startling images, to its final heart-stopping images, this late poem, written in the closing years of Thomas's life and published posthumously, carries a particular vibrancy, and shimmers with life. There is an intensity about the one who is shown to us, which seems to push some of the well-known themes just that bit further; and what unfolds is a vivid picture of a God who is, all at once, raw and explosive, hidden and visible, beyond our capacity to hear, flashing light through the world, and roaring silently: who is in all and around all.

The poem begins with a conundrum. 'That there is the unfamiliar' could suggest that Thomas is opening out a scene before us: it could be 'that – there!' as if he is pointing for us to see. But so too could this alert us to Thomas's idea that we are called to *infer* God's presence in our world; not prove it, or argue for it, but infer it from all we discover, seeing and reading it afresh, discovering that God *is* through our encounter with the unfamiliar. And alerting us to the 'unfamiliar' that is to come, Thomas invites us straight away into the

> ... landscape
> that will through all time
> resist our endeavours
> at domestication.

There is, he hints, the world we see but also the untameable ground of our world; the quickening principle, which hides in plain sight, and 'models his disguises / without a thought'. Whether this is thoughtlessly or beyond thought, is difficult to know, but either way might leave us with an impression that the 'one / who models his disguises', does not do so through an act of the will, but simply *is* present, unbidden and unseen, 'disguised' in the natural world. And just as this unnamed, hidden God is beyond direct vision, so too can the sound of God resonate outside the range of human hearing: it is, in fact, 'as natural' for this God to be unhearable as it is to be invisible, inhabiting the world at a frequency beyond human sight or hearing. Here Thomas reminds us of a long-standing image of his: the image of God present in the 'frequencies' all around us. The name of his 1978 collection of poems, this often-used image conjures up the contours of light and sound; the speed of events, and the spaces between events; the pulsing of messages; unseen power that lights and heats our world. And perhaps, in the reminder of 'frequencies', there is also the more ambiguous overtone of frequencies and the association with this of radiation (part of Thomas's ambivalent relationship with technology, in the final decades of the twentieth century), with its potential for good and ill. Here is an echo of Thomas's theme – his reminder to us – that the God who quickens us, and the life that vibrates around and within us, confounds any easy understanding.

As the poem travels on, these easy understandings are challenged more, and the intensity of God's power deepens and strengthens, as this invisible, hidden God bursts into life in plain sight, pouring through the world unbidden, unconfined and uncontrollable. Hiding in 'a seed', the Jack-in-the-box God jumps out at us, 'exploding / silently'. Unusually for Thomas, there is no break in the poem to signal this change: the mood shifts as silently and as surprisingly as the God who suddenly shocks us with explosive power:

> ... He hides himself
> in a seed so that exploding
> silently he pervades the world.

This is the God who erupts into growth, pouring verdant life into the world. This is the God whom we, wittingly or unwittingly, try to imprison under the flagstones of the paths we tread, but who 'escapes' from our clutches, untidies our paths, and in the 'haemorrhage / of raw flowers' pouring through the cracks reshapes our steps with a riot of colour. Life pours untidily through the world that we lay on top of God's world, and even though invisible, lights our way, with sometimes shocking intensity. In an image both benign and terrifying, Thomas's God

> ... bares his teeth
> in the lightening, delivering
> his electric bite.

Not lightning, we are told, but *lightening*; not lightening, we may hear, but *lightning*. Roaring through the sky, Thomas's God crackles through our lives, bringing light and energy, not smiling, but 'bar[ing] his teeth'. The God of love who quickens all life is also the God of power, not only revealed in hints, gentleness and soft air, but in raw, wild and shocking revelations. Here is the 'unfamiliar' that Thomas names at the beginning: the

> ... landscape
> that will through all time
> resist our endeavours
> at domestication.

And we are invited to catch a vision of this divine, undomesticated landscape, with God's hidden life suddenly laid bare, and revealed to us, not in visions or words; not in proofs, or apologetics, logic or theological formulations. The life that pours around and within, colourfully, pervasively, unbidden and untameable, is God's life, and is inferred from the clamour, tumult and glory of our world. But to be true to what we see, we are asked also to challenge our images of God. The 'evidence' of the world from which we infer God's vibrant presence calls us to resist easy, cosy images, and to embrace with wonder the vision of a God who also 'appals us / with his thunder'. The unnamed God of 'That there ...' may call us to worship, to surrender, to lift our vision, and to hear with Job, God calling out of the whirlwind, 'Where were you when I laid the foundation of the earth?'[81]

Finally, Thomas opens out a puzzling conundrum of an ending, which invites us further and deeper into the unfamiliar God who may be inferred even in the most startling of sources. This God, says Thomas,

> ... appals us
> with his thunder only to unnerve us
> further with the blessing of his held breath.

'The blessing of his held breath.' Where, I wonder, do these few words leave us? Their ambivalence may be heart-stopping, breath-taking, unsettling or even scary. But they may also invite us into a richness of association which draws us on, beyond the life of the poem, and on beyond our pictures and images of God. After the thunder, the winds are suddenly stilled, we may hear. Or the breath of life draws to a close; or we are held in an eternal in-breath, longing to breathe out into God's presence. Or simply, there is peace, unnerving in its depth.

That there is the unfamiliar as well as the familiar may unnerve us and will bless us.

Week 5 – Seeing

Day 7

The first king

The first king was on horseback.
The second a pillion rider.
The third came by plane.

Where was the god-child?
He was in the manger
with the beasts, all looking

the other way where the fourth
was a slow dawning because
wisdom must come on foot.

The first king

It might have been satisfying to draw these weeks of reflections to a close by pondering an unambiguously glorious poem of the Feast of the Epiphany, just ahead of us; a poem of manifestation and seeing in the season of showing. A rich vision of the kings, perhaps, come to worship with their gifts, or a heartbreaking exploration of the life-changing rigours of the journey, as in Eliot's magnificent *The Journey of the Magi*.[82] Typically with Thomas, however, what might be seen as conventional comforts are bound to elude us. Those poems of the Epiphany which are to be found in his poetry, twist and turn and leave us discomfited; for example, 'Epiphany', in the collection *Frequencies*.[83] An acerbic poem of 'showing' not the glory of Christ, but the folly of we who replace Him with 'tinsel' and 'toys', 'Epiphany' also plays with our relationship of Christ the newborn, and Christ the man, and our impulse at Christmas to domesticate this man who will hang from the cross, by placing Him at our dinner table, caught in the folly of our babe-less celebrations. In 'Lost Christmas',[84] three kings are briefly likened to three trees, foretelling Golgotha, and in 'Were you one of the three',[85] gifts of heart, mind and soul are brought to a mechanized manger, and we seem to be asked what we have come to have faith in, in our technological world.

And then there is this brief, bitter-sweet poem 'The first king', from Thomas's collection *Counterpoint*. This is also a disquieting, ambivalent poem, with a bit of a sting in the tale. But in this case, the 'sting' may not be as acid as usual. Perhaps, towards the end of it, it will have nudged us in a new direction, with a nugget of hopeful anticipation which might enrich the coming days as we look ahead to the epiphany. Fittingly, the poem begins with the arrival of three kings, who have travelled by increasingly contemporary and fast ways of journeying: the first comes by horse and the second is 'a pillion rider', on the back of a motorbike, and, finally, a third king arrives 'by plane'. We might assume they have come to pay homage out of humility, or offer gifts, according to the story of the three kings or wise men, but there is no sign of this, and there are no gifts to be found. There are only the ever-hastening approaches which hint not at humility, but at a greedy curiosity, perhaps the staking of some hungry claim on the Christ child.

And at their approaching, the god-child, we hear, is in the manger still, with the stable animals. But they, the vulnerable of Bethlehem, do not look towards those riding towards them, travelling at speed, gathering momentum through the centuries with increasingly sophisticated ways of travelling and at greater and greater speed. They look 'the other way' towards a different, more gradual approach: towards a traveller who arrives on foot, surrendering to a journey that is not about velocity but about growing in wisdom: towards a 'fourth', which is

... a slow dawning because
wisdom must come on foot.

Here is the 'sting' in the tail: a direct challenge to the increas-
ing speed of the kings, who hurtle their way to Bethlehem,
perhaps mirroring a contemporary illusion that speed of travel
is in itself a cause for celebration, and a way of arriving at a
destination of our dreams. But the Christ child is not subject
to illusions, and the nature of wisdom is revealed as a 'slow
dawning', not a rapid approach to the truth. This sting, then,
is turning the world the right way up.

There is an echo here of the story of *The Other Wise Man*,
by the clergyman, writer and diplomat, Henry Van Dyke.[86] In
1896 he published the story of a fourth wise man, Artaban,
who sets out to greet the newborn king, taking with him
precious jewels as gifts, including the 'pearl of great price'. But
stopping to help a dying man, his journey is delayed, and he
arrives in Bethlehem to find that the family of Jesus has fled.
And so Artaban searches for Jesus, and spends the next thirty-
three years travelling, called on by the child-turned-man whom
he has not seen, but continues to follow, forever drawn by the
lure of the godhead. And on the way he helps others, and grad-
ually uses up the treasures he had brought as gifts, including
the 'pearl of great price'. Finally, he arrives in Jerusalem at the
time of the crucifixion, and dies after a lifetime of following.
His is a slow journey, of a slow wise man, who never reaches
his 'goal' but is forever caught up in the gradual shaping of
faith and following. For him too there is a 'slow dawning,
because / wisdom must come on foot'.

As we come towards the end of these weeks of waiting,
accepting, journeying, birthing and seeing with R. S. Thomas
as our companion, we may be discovering that wisdom must
come on foot, as it did for Thomas. Through years of walking
the hills of Wales, he discovered a louring world transfigured
by God's presence, and a people worthy of respect whose lives
had endured through the wind and weather and God's grace.

But all this was years in the discovering, and to read Thomas's
poetry is to enter into his slow wisdom. It is to allow ourselves to

sit patiently, waiting upon the language to speak to us through its layers of possibility, and to wait upon the God who discovers us in the depths that are stirred and agitated within us. It is to accept our own limitations in understanding and placing the finite word upon infinite meaning, and it is travelling faithfully into a mystery that opens up before us. And to read Thomas as our companion is also to allow his vision of God's kingdom to come to birth within us, and to see the world afresh, as a layered, textured place: a place of revelation and presence; a place of grace and gift, discovered over time,

… because
wisdom must come on foot.

References

1 Thomas, 'Neb', in *R. S. Thomas: Autobiographies*, J. Walford Davies (trans., intro. and notes), Phoenix, 1997, p. 76.

2 Thomas, 'The Making of a Poem', in *R. S. Thomas: Selected Prose*, Sandra Anstey (ed.), Seren, 1995, p. 88.

3 George Herbert, 'The Flower'.

4 Thomas, *Song at the Year's Turning: Poems, 1942–1954*, Rupert Hart-Davis, 1955; published when he was the rector of Eglwysfach in mid-Wales.

5 Thomas, 'Neb', *Autobiographies*, p. 76.

6 Thomas, 'Kneeling', in *Not That He Brought Flowers*, Rupert Hart-Davis, 1968.

7 Thomas, 'Neb', *Autobiographies*, p. 76.

8 Genesis 28.16.

9 R. S. Thomas as priest in 'Kneeling' is very different from R. S. Thomas as priest 20 years before in 'A Priest to His People', in which he faced the congregation with the power of God behind him, haranguing them in confused exasperation at their failure to find God in the aesthetics of the Church.

10 Thomas wrote two poems with this name. This one is from *Laboratories of the Spirit*, Macmillan, 1975.

11 George Herbert, 'Prayer'.

12 This is the second of Thomas's poems called 'Suddenly', in *Later Poems: 1972–1982*, Macmillan, 1983.

13 Acts 2.1–13: the apostles are 'filled with the Holy Spirit and began to speak in other languages', and so can be understood. Acts 10.44–48: God's Spirit is poured out on the Gentiles in Joppa while Peter is speaking and 'the circumcised believers who had come with Peter were astounded that the gift of the Holy Spirit had been poured out even among the Gentiles'.

14 Iago Prytherch appears in many of Thomas's poems, from 'A Peasant' and 'Iago Prytherch', in his earliest volume *The Stones of the Field* (The Druid Press Ltd, 1946), to 'Servant', in *The Bread of Truth* (Rupert Hart-Davis, 1963), and 'Gone?', in *Frequencies* (Macmillan, 1978). All in R. S. Thomas, *Collected Poems, 1945–1990*, J. M. Dent & Sons, 1994.

15 Thomas, 'The Paths Gone By', *R. S. Thomas: Selected Prose*, p. 100.

16 Thomas, 'Neb', *Autobiographies*, p. 74.

17 Thomas, 'Neb', *Autobiographies*, p. 65.

18 Thomas, 'Neb', *Autobiographies*, p. 77.

19 Thomas, *The Echoes Return Slow*, Macmillan, 1988; Thomas, *R. S. Thomas: Collected Later Poems, 1988–2000*, Bloodaxe Books, 2004.

20 John A. T. Robinson, *Honest to God*, SCM Press, 1963, p. 19.

21 Robinson, *Honest to God*, p. 87.

22 'R. S. Thomas: Priest and Poet', film by John Ormond, introduced by Sam Adams, BBC Television, 2 April 1972, transcript in *Poetry Wales*, Spring, 1972, p. 51.

23 From the Anglican Catechism in the Book of Common Prayer: www.churchofengland.org/prayer-and-worship/worship-texts-and-resources/book-common-prayer/catechism.

24 From *Where do we go from here?*, 1974; and published in *Selected Prose*, pp. 120–1.

25 'R. S. Thomas: Priest and Poet', film by Ormond, *Poetry Wales*.

26 Matthew 13.45–46.

27 Exodus 3.2–6.

28 Matthew 6.10.

29 This poem was published in *Laboratories of the Spirit* (1975); and the other in *Frequencies* (1978).

30 'An Interview with R. S. Thomas', *Daily Telegraph*, 4 December 1999.

31 There are strong echoes here of T. S. Eliot, Part V of 'The Dry Salvages', in *Four Quartets*, Faber & Faber, 2001.

32 In 'Neb', Thomas often refers to the birds he sees around him (e.g. pp. 91 and 95) and he mentions trips he made with Elsi in 1968 to Norway and to Mallorca to go bird-watching. He also travelled within Britain to see birds, as Grevel Lindop describes in *An Afternoon with R. S. Thomas*, https://grevel.co.uk/poetry/an-afternoon-with-r-s-thomas/.

33 Thomas, 'A Year in Llŷn', in *Autobiographies*.

34 One of the very few poems he repeated. It also appeared as an unnamed poem in *Counterpoint*, Bloodaxe Books, 1990.

35 www.pilgrims-way-north-wales.org/index.html.

36 Diarmaid MacCulloch, *A History of Christianity: The First Three Thousand Years*, Penguin, 2009, p. 332.

37 Robinson, *Honest to God*, p. 47.

38 Edward Howells talks about 'unsaying' as a way of speaking about God through 'affirmation and negation, with an emphasis on the negative element', to point to God's 'transcendence of all human language'. E. Howells, 'Apophatic Spirituality', in *The New SCM*

Dictionary of Christian Spirituality, SCM Press, 2013, p. 117. Michael Sells talks about 'un-saying or speaking away', as a way of describing the ineffable in Sells, *Mystical Languages of Unsaying*, University of Chicago Press, 1994, pp. 2–3.

39 Stephen Hawking, *A Brief History Of Time: From Big Bang to Black Holes*, Transworld, Kindle Edition, p. 92.

40 Hawking, *A Brief History Of Time*, p. 104.

41 Denys Turner, *The Darkness of God: Negativity in Christian Mysticism*, Cambridge University Press, 1995, p. 20.

42 W. B. Yeats, 'The Second Coming', in *Michael Robartes and the Dancer*, 1921.

43 The World Egg is a commonly held image of creation. In Greek mythology, the egg is usually depicted with a snake wound around it. In Thomas's time, the image became current again. Robert Graves in *The Greek Myths* (Penguin, 2017) wrote of the serpent Ophion wound seven times around the Cosmic Egg for incubation, and physics and cosmology hinted at a dramatic 'hatching' in the big bang.

44 She has been called a 'female Celtic Saint', www.ithonvalley parishes.com/llananno.html, or 'St Anno, Annu, Wanna or Wonno', who may have been male or female, or even St Anne, the mother of the Virgin Mary, in *The Journal of Antiquities*, https://thejournalofantiquities. com/2013/07/18/st-annos-church-llananno-powys-wales/.

45 A photograph of the rood screen can be seen on the Llananno page of the Visit Wales website: www.visitwales.com/attraction-search/ attraction-search-results/attraction-search-details?id=1843127.

46 For example, Thomas: 'Christmas', in *Pietà* (Rupert Hart-Davis, 1967); 'Song', in *H'm* (Macmillan, 1972); 'Lost Christmas', in *Young and Old* (Chatto & Windus, 1972); 'Hill Christmas' from *Laboratories of the Spirit* (Macmillan, 1975); 'Carol', in *Later Poems* (Macmillan, 1984); or 'Festival' in *Residues* (Bloodaxe Books, 2002).

47 Sells, *Mystical Languages of Unsaying*, p. 3.

48 John Coulson paraphrases Wittgenstein in Coulson, *Religion and Imagination: In Aid of a Grammar of Assent*, Clarendon Press, 1981, p. 27.

49 Examples include some of the unnamed poems in Thomas, *Counterpoint*, which begin: 'The Nativity? No', 'Were you one of the three?' and 'Come closer'. 'Lost Christmas', in *Young and Old*; and 'The Cones' in *Later Poems* are also examples of the familiar landscape of the nativity turned aside to offer a different picture.

50 For example, in *The Echoes Return Slow*, Macmillan, 1988; and in *Collected Later Poems, 1988–2000*.

51 Thomas, 'A Frame for Poetry', *Selected Prose*.

52 To find out more about how metaphor and symbol can be understood in this way, see Coulson *Religion and Imagination*, p. 36.

53 The first quote is from an interview with Simon Barker in an

unpublished dissertation: 'Probing the God-Space: R S Thomas's Poetry of Religious Experience with special reference to Kierkegaard', PhD thesis, University of Wales (Lampeter), 1991, Appendix II, interview 309–310. The second is from 'R. S. Thomas: Priest and Poet', film by Ormond, *Poetry Wales*, p. 53.

54 In his 1981 collection *Between Here and Now*. See also the 1985 collection *Ingrowing Thoughts*.

55 As Thomas wrote two poems called 'Emerging', this one, from the 1978 collection *Frequencies*, will be called 'Emerging (1978)' to distinguish it from the earlier 'Emerging', from the 1975 collection *Laboratories of the Spirit*.

56 An often-quoted vision of Michelangelo. In *The Story of Art* (Phaidon, 1984), E. H. Gombrich tells how Michelangelo had the overwhelming experience in the marble quarries of Carrera of 'wanting to release the figures from the stones in which they were slumbering' (p. 231).

57 Robinson, p. 13. John Robinson's *Honest to God*, which brought to a wide readership the idea that God might be re-imagined in depth as well as in distance, is still in Thomas's library in the University College of North Wales, Bangor.

58 Andrew Davison says that 'our word "Mass" comes from something rather close to "Off with you! Out you go! You've got work to do!"' Davison, *Why Sacraments?* SPCK, 2013, p. 24.

59 William Temple, 'The Sacramental Universe', *Nature, Man and God, Gifford Lectures*, 1932–33 and 1933–34, MacMillan & Co. Ltd, 1964, lecture XIX, p. 478.

60 Henry Vaughan's poem *The Night* can be found on the Poetry Foundation website at www.poetryfoundation.org/poems/50441/the-night-56d22d9009233.

61 J. Robert Barth, *The Symbolic Imagination: Coleridge and the Romantic Tradition*, Princeton University Press, 1977, p. 11.

62 This the second poem which Thomas wrote with this name. The first poem called 'The Gap', appeared in *Laboratories of the Spirit*.

63 The Tower of Babel (Genesis 11.1–9) tells how humanity decided to build a tower reaching heavenwards. God, recognizing in this the threat of human dominance, confuses their previously common speech so that language is no longer shared, and the threat receded.

64 'Thing-in-itself' is Kant's expression for 'the object considered as it is independently of its cognitive relation to the human mind' in contrast with the appearance of an object: H. E. Allison, 'Thing-in-itself', in Ted Honderich (ed.), *The Oxford Companion to Philosophy*, Oxford University Press, 1995, p. 871.

65 'R. S. Thomas: Priest and Poet', film by Ormond, *Poetry Wales*, p. 55.

66 'Neb', *Autobiographies*, p. 103.

67 'Neb', *Autobiographies*, p. 103.

68 'Once', 'The Island' and 'He', all in *H'm*; 'The Sea', in *Young and Old*. All in R. S. Thomas, *Collected Poems, 1945–1990*.

69 'The Other', 'Sea-watching', in *Laboratories of the Spirit*; 'Pilgrimages', in *Between Here and Now*. All in R. S. Thomas: *Collected Poems 1945–90*.

70 Thomas, *The Echoes Return Slow*; Thomas, *R. S. Thomas: Collected Later Poems, 1988–2000*.

71 Thomas described 'Neb', how Prytherch came into being. '[O]n a dark, cold day in November, on his way to visit a family in a farm over a thousand feet above sea-level, he saw the farmer's brother out in the field, docking mangels', p. 52. He also referred to this in his *Letters to Raymond Garlick* (15 March 1969, p. 75).

72 All published in *R. S. Thomas: Collected Poems 1945–90*.

73 In *The Bread of Truth*. Also in R. S. Thomas, *Collected Poems, 1945–1990*.

74 Sells, *Mystical Languages of Unsaying*, p. 207.

75 This is one of Thomas's ways of understanding God. Thomas drew consciously from Paul Tillich to express this. 'I do like Tillich's idea of the Ground of Being, that is God is not a being,' he said in a BBC Radio interview: *R. S. Thomas at Seventy*, presented by Kevin Crossley-Holland, BBC Radio 3, London, 7 December 1983, transcript; M. J. J. van Buuren, *Waiting: The Religious Poetry of Ronald Stuart Thomas, Welsh Poet and Priest*, Katholieke Universitat van Nijmegen, 1993, p. 178.

76 Quoted by Thomas in 'A Frame for Poetry', *Selected Prose*, Anstey 71. The quote is from Allen Tate, 'The Symbolic Imagination', in *Essays in Four Decades*, Oxford University Press, 1970, p. 431.

77 Coulson, *Religion and Imagination*, p. 10. There are also echoes of Anya Taylor's ideas about Coleridge's primary and secondary imaginations: John Beer (gen. ed.), *Coleridge's Writings*, Vol. 2, Anya Taylor (ed.), *On Humanity*, St Martin's Press, 1994, p. 220.

78 R. S. Thomas, Introduction, *The Penguin Book of Religious Verse*, Penguin, 1963, p. 8. My italics. Here Thomas is drawing on Coleridge's ideas about the 'primary imagination' as the creative force of God: S. T. Coleridge, *Bibliographia Literaria*, or *Biographical Sketches of My Literary Life and Opinions*, James Engell and W. Jackson Bate (eds), 1983, CC Vol. 7, BL I, Princeton University Press, 1984, pp. 304–5.

79 Thomas, Introduction, *The Penguin Book of Religious Verse*, p. 8.

80 For example, see 'Dialectic', and 'At It', both in *Frequencies* and published in *R. S. Thomas: Collected Poems 1945–90*.

81 Job 38.4.

82 T. S. Eliot, 'The Journey of the Magi', *The Complete Poems and Plays of T. S. Eliot*, Faber and Faber, 1969.

83 'Epiphany', in *Collected Poems, 1945–1990*.

84 'Lost Christmas', from *Young and Old* and in *Collected Poems, 1945–1990*.

85 'Were you one of the three', from *Counterpoint* and in *Collected Later Poems, 1988–2000*.

86 Henry Van Dyke, *The Other Wise Man*, Harper and Brothers, 1896.

Acknowledgement of Sources

Reproduced by kind permission of Orion Books:
'The Coming', 'In a Country Church', 'In Church', 'Kneeling', 'Suddenly' (1975), 'Suddenly' (1983), 'Sea-watching', 'Amen', 'This to do', 'The Moor', 'The Bright Field', 'Emerging' (1975), 'In Context', 'Pilgrimages', 'The Moon in Lleyn', 'Llananno', 'Emerging' (1978), 'The Gap' (1978), 'The Kingdom', 'The Absence', 'Adjustments', all in R. S. Thomas, *Collected Poems, 1945–1990*, J. M. Dent & Sons, 1994.

Reproduced by kind permission of Bloodaxe Books:
'The first king', 'The imperatives of the instincts', 'I know him', 'Top left an angel', 'Other incarnations, of course', 'Tidal', 'Migrants', 'Wrong?', 'Evening', 'Blind Noel', 'Nativity', 'The Un-born', 'The God' and 'That there …', all in R. S. Thomas, *Collected Later Poems, 1988–2000*, Bloodaxe Books, 2004.